A COMPREHENSIVE GUI[illegible]
GOVERNMENT

MW01443307

TABLE OF CONTENTS

Chapter 1: Introduction to ChatGPT for Government
This chapter gives a broad overview of ChatGPT, including its benefits, limitations, and potential applications in the government sector. Topics include AI ethics, data security, and technological literacy. It sets the groundwork for subsequent chapters by outlining the scope of this guide.

Chapter 2: Setting Up ChatGPT in Government Systems
In this chapter, we discuss technical aspects of setting up ChatGPT for use in government systems, such as integration with existing infrastructure, compliance with regulatory standards, data handling procedures, and security considerations.

Chapter 3: Privacy, Security, and Ethical Considerations
This chapter delves deeper into the ethical and security implications of AI use in government. We cover principles of responsible AI usage, ensuring user privacy, anonymizing and handling sensitive data, dealing with AI bias, and promoting transparency in AI systems.

Chapter 4: ChatGPT for Internal Communications
Explore the various ways in which ChatGPT can be leveraged for internal government communications, such as minute-taking, drafting correspondence, facilitating brainstorming sessions, and training government personnel.

Chapter 5: ChatGPT for Citizen Interaction
This chapter focuses on using ChatGPT as an interface between the government and citizens, providing services such as citizen inquiries, public service automation, and sentiment analysis on public opinion.

Chapter 6: ChatGPT in Policy Making
Here, we discuss how ChatGPT can be used to assist in policy-making processes, including information gathering, policy drafting, and simulating policy outcomes based on large sets of data.

Chapter 7: Monitoring and Evaluation of ChatGPT Use
This chapter guides on ways to assess the effectiveness and efficiency of ChatGPT in government use. Topics covered include setting key performance indicators, regular auditing, feedback collection, and continual improvement of AI systems.

Chapter 8: Training and Capacity Building
Training government personnel to use ChatGPT effectively is essential. This chapter covers developing training programs, addressing skill gaps, and promoting an AI-positive culture within the government.

Chapter 9: Future Scenarios and Predictions
This chapter focuses on the future possibilities of ChatGPT in government, drawing from current trends and technological advancements. It will highlight the potential role of ChatGPT in areas like disaster management, education, healthcare, and more.

Chapter 10: Conclusion and Next Steps

The final chapter sums up the key points discussed in previous chapters. It provides guidance on formulating a roadmap for ChatGPT implementation, maintaining the system, and iterating improvements based on experiences and outcomes.

INTRODUCTION TO THE GUIDE: HARNESSING THE POWER OF CHATGPT IN GOVERNMENT OPERATIONS

Welcome to this comprehensive guide that seeks to demystify the integration of advanced Artificial Intelligence (AI) technologies, specifically OpenAI's ChatGPT, into government operations. As we delve deeper into the 21st century, AI has increasingly become a pivotal tool in transforming service delivery, policy-making, and citizen engagement in public sectors around the globe. This guide serves as a roadmap, highlighting the potential of ChatGPT in revolutionizing governmental functions, along with providing actionable insights into the deployment, monitoring, and continuous improvement of AI systems.

Artificial Intelligence has the potential to greatly enhance efficiency, decision-making capabilities, and user engagement within government operations. ChatGPT, a powerful language model developed by OpenAI, stands at the forefront of this revolution. With its ability to generate human-like text based on the input it receives, it presents numerous opportunities to streamline service delivery, improve citizen interaction, and optimize internal processes within government settings.

However, the implementation of AI in government is not without challenges. From setting up the right infrastructure to training personnel, ensuring ethical use, and addressing concerns related to privacy and security, there's a lot to consider. This guide will navigate you through these complexities, presenting step-by-step procedures, best practices, and vital considerations for effective AI implementation.

From discussing the potential applications and benefits of ChatGPT in Chapter 1 to exploring key concerns and guidelines for Responsible AI in Chapter 3, this guide takes a deep dive into all the essential aspects of integrating ChatGPT into government operations. Subsequent chapters detail the process of setting up the infrastructure, training, monitoring, and the future of AI in government.

Whether you're a government leader seeking to understand how AI can improve your department's operations, a policy-maker exploring how to integrate AI ethically and effectively, or an AI enthusiast keen to understand the potential of AI in public service, this guide offers valuable insights for everyone. As we venture into the new age of government operations, this guide seeks to aid you in harnessing the power of AI for the public good. Let's embark on this exciting journey together!

CHAPTER 1: INTRODUCTION TO CHATGPT FOR GOVERNMENT

This chapter gives a broad overview of ChatGPT, including its benefits, limitations, and potential applications in the government sector. Topics include AI ethics, data security, and technological literacy. It sets the groundwork for subsequent chapters by outlining the scope of this guide.

Artificial Intelligence (AI) is a field of computer science that aims to create machines that mimic human intelligence - learning, reasoning, problem-solving, perception, and language-understanding capabilities. Over the past decades, AI technology has matured and proliferated to various sectors, significantly changing the landscape of business, healthcare, entertainment, and now increasingly, government operations. The capabilities offered by AI are unprecedented, from handling massive data sets and making predictive analyses to facilitating real-time decision making and automating routine tasks.

One specific branch of AI, Machine Learning (ML), has proven particularly impactful. ML algorithms enable machines to learn from data and improve their performance without being explicitly programmed to do so. This feature is at the heart of OpenAI's GPT and its derivatives, including ChatGPT.

The GPT series, standing for Generative Pretrained Transformer, is a state-of-the-art AI model for understanding and generating human-like text. It's pretrained on a large corpus of text data and can generate coherent and contextually relevant sentences by predicting the likelihood of a word given the previous words used in the text. This results in remarkably human-like text generation, with the capacity to write essays, answer questions, and even engage in conversation.

ChatGPT, a version of the GPT model specifically fine-tuned for conversational purposes, has been widely adopted across sectors for its powerful text generation capabilities. Businesses use it for customer service, educators use it as a teaching assistant, and creatives use it for brainstorming and content creation. The versatility and efficiency of ChatGPT make it a transformative tool for any entity that heavily relies on communication and information processing, including government.

Governments, given their scale and scope of responsibilities, stand to benefit significantly from AI technology like ChatGPT. By incorporating AI into its operations, a government can improve service delivery by automating responses to citizen inquiries, ensuring consistent and prompt service. This would allow for a more efficient allocation of human resources, freeing staff from routine tasks and allowing them to focus on complex problems that require human judgment and expertise.

AI can also enhance policy-making processes. ChatGPT can assist in policy drafting by providing suggestions based on a vast dataset of policy documents. It can also simulate policy outcomes based on historical data, helping policymakers understand the potential impacts of their decisions before implementation.

Furthermore, ChatGPT can help facilitate citizen engagement. Governments could use the tool to gain insights into public sentiment, analyze citizen feedback, or automate public communications. This could help governments stay attuned to their constituents' needs and respond to them more effectively.

In conclusion, AI, particularly models like ChatGPT, offer exciting opportunities to revolutionize government operations. But while the potential benefits are vast, careful planning and strategic implementation are needed to ensure that the technology is used responsibly and ethically. With appropriate safeguards and training in place, governments can harness AI to deliver more efficient and effective public services.

ChatGPT is a state-of-the-art language model developed by OpenAI, designed to generate text that mimics human conversation or prose. As a product of machine learning, specifically a variant called transformer-based deep learning, it has the remarkable ability to produce text that not only appears grammatically correct and fluent but also maintains context and provides meaningful responses.

One of the unique features of ChatGPT is its ability to generate human-like text based on the input it receives. It can comprehend a prompt, carry the context forward, and generate a response accordingly. This capability makes it a powerful tool for a variety of applications including answering queries, writing essays, summarizing lengthy documents, translating between languages, and even composing poetry or stories. This wide-ranging applicability is a direct result of its extensive pre-training on diverse internet text and the ability to learn patterns, context, and nuances within the language.

This text-generation ability has significant implications for the range of tasks that ChatGPT can perform. As long as a task involves textual data or communication, ChatGPT has potential applicability. For example, it can be used to draft emails or other forms of correspondence, automate report writing, aid in documentation, provide summaries of long meetings or discussions, etc.

When considering the vast array of responsibilities governments handle, the integration of an AI model like

ChatGPT can be particularly advantageous. Government agencies manage a multitude of tasks that involve text processing and document handling. From drafting policy documents and legal texts to processing public inquiries and issuing public communications, text forms an integral part of the government's daily operations.

ChatGPT can potentially streamline many of these processes, making them more efficient and freeing up human resources for tasks that require critical thinking, decision-making, and personal interactions. For instance, ChatGPT can be used to automate responses to standard public inquiries, allowing government staff to focus on more complex and unique cases.

In policy drafting, ChatGPT can provide assistance by producing initial drafts or suggesting modifications based on pre-existing policy documents. In internal communication, it can aid in the creation of memos, briefing notes, and meeting minutes, easing the burden of these often time-consuming tasks.

In summary, the integration of ChatGPT within government systems has the potential to significantly enhance productivity, speed up service delivery, and improve the overall efficiency of governmental operations. However, this also necessitates careful planning and strategic implementation to ensure responsible and ethical use of the technology. This includes comprehensive training for personnel, maintaining transparency in AI usage, ensuring data privacy, and regularly monitoring and updating the system to address any potential issues or biases.

While the benefits of integrating ChatGPT within government operations are significant, it is also essential to examine the potential limitations and challenges associated with this technological adoption. These hurdles mainly revolve around three critical areas: ethical considerations, data privacy and security, and technical literacy requirements.

Ethical Considerations

AI systems, including ChatGPT, operate based on the data they are trained on. As such, they may unintentionally inherit and perpetuate the biases present in their training data. In a government context, such bias can lead to unfair outcomes and a lack of equity in public service delivery, policy-making, and citizen engagement. Therefore, implementing ChatGPT ethically requires careful handling of its training and usage, with constant monitoring to detect and correct potential bias.

Moreover, while AI can automate many tasks, there are ethical implications around decisions that require human judgment, empathy, and understanding of complex social contexts. It's crucial to establish boundaries on what tasks are appropriate for AI and which ones should be reserved for human agents.

Data Privacy and Security

Governments manage an immense amount of data, much of it sensitive and confidential. When incorporating AI systems like ChatGPT into government operations, ensuring the privacy and security of this data is paramount. This involves not only secure data handling and storage but also careful management of how data is used by the AI. For instance, while ChatGPT can provide anonymized and aggregated data analysis, it should not be used in a way that risks exposing individuals' personal information.

Moreover, as an AI system connected to the internet, ChatGPT could potentially be a target for cyber-attacks. Governments must ensure robust cybersecurity measures are in place to protect against such threats.

Technical Literacy Requirements

Implementing ChatGPT effectively in the public sector requires a certain level of technical literacy among both government personnel and citizens. For government staff, this involves understanding how to use the system, interpret its outputs, and monitor its performance. It may also involve knowing how to troubleshoot issues or work with technical support to resolve more complex problems.

For citizens, while ChatGPT is designed to interact in a user-friendly, conversational manner, there may still be a learning curve, particularly for those less familiar with digital technologies. Therefore, it's crucial to provide accessible instructions and support to ensure all citizens can benefit from this new tool.

Addressing these challenges requires careful planning, clear policies, ongoing training, and a commitment to transparency and accountability. Despite these challenges, the potential benefits of ChatGPT in enhancing government operations and citizen services are significant. As we navigate the chapters of this guide, we will provide detailed discussions and solutions to these challenges to assist government entities in harnessing the power of AI responsibly and effectively.

Processing Vast Amounts of Data

One of the distinguishing features of ChatGPT, and indeed many AI models, is its ability to process, analyze, and learn from vast quantities of data with speed and accuracy far surpassing human capabilities. This feature has considerable implications for a range of government functions that involve large-scale data management.

For instance, government agencies often handle a high volume of public inquiries daily. Managing this traffic effectively and providing prompt responses can be a challenge. Here, ChatGPT can significantly enhance service delivery. By rapidly processing and responding to standard inquiries, the AI can ensure quicker response times and more consistent information provision, improving overall citizen satisfaction.

Document Analysis and Policy Making

Government operations also involve the generation and analysis of large volumes of documents, from policy documents and legal texts to reports and meeting minutes. Manually analyzing these texts can be time-consuming and error-prone. ChatGPT, with its capacity for rapid text analysis and summary, can assist in this process, providing overviews, extracting key points, and even identifying patterns or trends over time.

In policy-making, ChatGPT's ability to analyze vast data sets can be harnessed to provide insights and projections based on historical data. It can assist in simulating policy outcomes, enabling decision-makers to make more informed choices.

Sentiment Analysis on Public Opinion

Understanding public sentiment is crucial for effective governance. Here too, ChatGPT can play a key role. By analyzing public communications, social media posts, and feedback, the AI can provide sentiment analysis on a scale that would be challenging manually. This can help governments understand public opinion on various issues, guiding policy decisions, and public communication strategies.

Streamlining Internal Operations

Internally, ChatGPT can automate various routine tasks, freeing up staff to focus on more complex, critical activities. For example, it can assist in drafting communications, generating initial drafts based on input parameters, or providing suggestions to improve existing drafts.

ChatGPT can also aid in transcribing meetings, ensuring accurate record-keeping without the need for manual transcription. Moreover, it can automate aspects of project management, such as scheduling, tracking progress, or generating updates.

In conclusion, ChatGPT's capacity to handle and analyze vast amounts of data, coupled with its versatile text generation capabilities, makes it a powerful tool for enhancing government services and streamlining operations. However, the effective implementation of such technology requires careful planning, staff training, and robust policies to ensure ethical use and data security. As this guide continues, we will delve into these considerations, offering comprehensive guidance for governments looking to harness the power of AI.

Deploying AI tools such as ChatGPT in public sector operations indeed poses several ethical considerations. The main concerns arise in areas such as data privacy, transparency, equity, and accountability. Given the government's responsibility to uphold the highest ethical standards in serving the public interest, these considerations must be carefully addressed in the process of AI integration.

Data Privacy

The government manages a vast array of data, much of it sensitive. While AI tools like ChatGPT do not store personal data after the conversation ends or use it to inform future conversations, the mere process of inputting data into the system for processing raises privacy considerations. As such, strict protocols need to be implemented to determine what data can be fed into the

AI system, with anonymization measures wherever necessary.

Transparency

Transparency is an ethical necessity when AI is used in government operations. Citizens have a right to know when and how AI tools are being used in the delivery of public services. For instance, if ChatGPT is used to respond to citizen inquiries, it should be clearly communicated that the interaction involves an AI system.

Equity and Bias

AI systems learn from the data they are trained on. If the training data contains biases, the AI system can unintentionally inherit and amplify these biases in its outputs. For instance, if the AI is trained on historical policy documents, it might reinforce outdated or biased policy perspectives.

In the context of government operations, such potential bias can have severe implications, leading to inequitable outcomes in public service delivery or decision-making processes. Governments need to ensure that the datasets used to train and fine-tune ChatGPT are as unbiased and representative as possible. Regular audits and updates are necessary to ensure the AI system continues to operate equitably.

Accountability

When AI systems are involved in public service delivery, it can create complexities around accountability. Even though an AI model like ChatGPT can generate responses, the ultimate responsibility for the provided service or decision lies with the government. There should be clear mechanisms to hold human overseers accountable for the outcomes of AI-assisted processes.

In conclusion, while ChatGPT can be a powerful tool in enhancing government operations, its deployment needs to be underpinned by a robust ethical framework. Governments need to ensure that their use of AI upholds the principles of privacy, transparency, equity, and accountability. It's also important to note that AI tools like ChatGPT should augment human decision-making, not replace it, particularly in contexts that require empathy, discretion, and complex social understanding. Ethical deployment of AI in the public sector, therefore, involves not just careful planning and policy-making, but also ongoing monitoring, evaluation, and adjustment.

Data security is indeed a critical concern when integrating AI tools like ChatGPT into government operations. Government databases contain an enormous amount of sensitive information, including personal data of citizens, business records, health records, and other confidential information. When this data interacts with AI systems, there's a potential risk of data breaches, unauthorized access, and misuse of information if strict security measures are not in place.

Secure Data Handling and Anonymization

ChatGPT does not store personal data after the conversation ends, nor does it use this data to inform future conversations, according to the operational protocols set by OpenAI as of the last update in September 2021. Despite this, during an active interaction, sensitive information might be fed into the system. To mitigate potential risks, governments must establish clear guidelines and protocols about what type of data can be inputted into ChatGPT. Personal and sensitive data should be anonymized whenever possible before any AI interaction, ensuring the protection of citizen privacy.

Robust Cybersecurity Measures

As an AI model connected to the internet, ChatGPT could potentially become a target for cyber-attacks. This necessitates the need for robust cybersecurity measures in place, such as firewalls, secure servers, data encryption, two-factor authentication, and regular system updates to protect against any new threats.

Data Access Control

Access to AI systems and the data they process should be limited to authorized personnel only, with strict access control mechanisms in place. This includes measures like role-based access, where different users have varying levels of access depending on their role and need for information.

Regular Audits and Updates

Regular security audits should be conducted to identify and fix any potential vulnerabilities in the system. The audits should cover both the AI system and the wider IT infrastructure to ensure that any security loopholes are identified and fixed. Additionally, the AI system and security protocols should be regularly updated to respond to evolving threats and new developments in the field of AI and cybersecurity.

In conclusion, data security is a critical element in the ethical deployment of AI tools like ChatGPT in government operations. While the AI system offers immense potential in improving service delivery and decision-making, it should not compromise the privacy and security of citizen data. By adhering to strict security protocols, governments can protect their data while effectively harnessing the power of AI.

The deployment of AI tools like ChatGPT indeed brings about a shift in the necessary skills within government workforces. While these models promise a multitude of benefits in efficiency and capability, they are dependent on the technical literacy of those tasked with their operation. Thus, it becomes essential to equip staff with the necessary training and knowledge to ensure they can effectively use, manage, and troubleshoot these tools.

Staff Training and Capacity Building

Adopting ChatGPT within government operations requires a certain degree of proficiency in managing AI models. This does not mean everyone needs to be an AI expert. However, staff need to understand the basics of how

ChatGPT operates, what it can and cannot do, how to interact with it, and how to interpret its outputs.

Moreover, given the need for oversight and potential troubleshooting, there should be a subset of staff who have a deeper understanding of ChatGPT. These individuals would be responsible for monitoring the system, identifying and rectifying issues, and liaising with technical support if needed.

To this end, governments will need to invest in comprehensive training programs to improve their workforce's technical literacy. These could include workshops, e-learning courses, or on-the-job training.

Citizen Literacy

In addition to the government staff, consideration must also be given to the end-users, the citizens. Particularly in scenarios where ChatGPT is used in public-facing roles, such as handling public inquiries or delivering public services, there's a need to ensure citizens understand they are interacting with an AI model and how to engage with it effectively.

This could involve clear communication about the use of AI in public services, guidance on how to interact with the AI system, and providing support for users who might struggle with the digital interface.

Promoting an AI-Friendly Culture

Beyond specific training and capacity-building measures, it's also beneficial to promote a broader culture of digital literacy and innovation within government organizations. This can help foster a more accepting and proactive approach towards adopting new technologies like ChatGPT. This could be achieved through regular tech updates, discussions around digital innovation, or encouraging staff to experiment with new digital tools.

In conclusion, while the technical literacy required for using ChatGPT and similar AI tools may seem daunting at first, it's a manageable challenge with the right investment in training and capacity building. By fostering an AI-friendly culture and providing the necessary support, governments can ensure that their staff and citizens are equipped to take full advantage of the benefits offered by AI tools.

In this comprehensive guide, our goal is to provide a thorough understanding of how governments can effectively and ethically use AI tools like ChatGPT. The integration of AI into government operations is an evolving field with immense potential, but it also poses significant challenges. By offering a deep dive into these challenges and their possible solutions, we aim to pave the way for successful AI implementations within the public sector.

Setting Up ChatGPT in Government Systems

In the following chapters, we will begin by discussing the practical aspects of implementing ChatGPT within government systems. This involves setting up the technical infrastructure, integrating the AI with existing systems, ensuring data compatibility, and adhering to the necessary security protocols.

Applications of ChatGPT in Government

We will also explore the various applications of ChatGPT across different areas of government operation. From public service delivery and policy-making to internal communication and process automation, we'll provide a detailed look at how ChatGPT can enhance efficiency and effectiveness in these contexts.

Monitoring and Evaluation Strategies

Moreover, given the crucial importance of ethics and accountability in government operations, we will cover strategies for monitoring and evaluating the use of ChatGPT. This includes setting up robust oversight mechanisms, conducting regular audits, and ensuring transparency and accountability in AI-assisted processes.

Future Use Cases and Developments

Looking to the future, we will discuss emerging trends and potential advancements in AI, and how they might further influence government operations. As AI continues to evolve, it is likely to open up new possibilities for its application within the government sector.

By understanding the potentials and pitfalls of AI in government, it is possible to chart a course that harnesses this powerful tool for the public good, while minimizing its risks. As we delve into this fascinating field, we invite you to join us on this journey towards the future of governance.

Through this guide, we aim to facilitate a comprehensive understanding of the potentials and challenges of ChatGPT in government. By the end, we hope to leave you with a deep understanding of how to effectively and ethically harness the power of ChatGPT, and AI in general, for the betterment of public service delivery and governance.

Examples:

1. Citizen Inquiry Response System:
Background: Many government departments worldwide handle vast numbers of public inquiries daily, ranging from tax questions to health information and more. With thousands of emails and phone calls, manual responses become time-consuming and can lead to delays.
Implementation: Using ChatGPT, a municipal government integrated an AI-driven chatbot into its official website. This chatbot could respond in real-time to a wide range of public queries. It was trained on a dataset of frequently asked questions and historical responses, allowing it to provide relevant and accurate answers.
Outcome: The immediate availability of information significantly reduced wait times for citizens, and the burden on government staff was considerably lessened. Additionally, the system was able to gather data on the most frequently asked questions, allowing the department to proactively address citizen concerns in official communications.

2. Policy Drafting Assistance:
Background: Drafting policies can be a tedious process that involves examining existing legislation, ensuring alignment with international norms, and avoiding contradictions with current laws.
Implementation: A national legislative body incorporated ChatGPT into their drafting process. By feeding the system with existing legislation, lawmakers could quickly reference older laws, examine potential contradictions, and generate drafts more efficiently.
Outcome: The policy drafting became more streamlined, with fewer oversight errors, leading to more robust and comprehensive legislation.

3. Virtual Civic Education Tutor:
Background: With the increasing need for civic education, governments aim to ensure citizens are well-informed about their rights, responsibilities, and the workings of their institutions.
Implementation: A Ministry of Education, in partnership with local schools, launched a ChatGPT-powered virtual tutor. This tutor, available on a dedicated platform, provided information about the nation's constitution, legislative processes, and more.
Outcome: Students and the general public, especially those without immediate access to traditional education resources, had a readily available and interactive source of civic education.

4. Translation and Language Services:
Background: In multilingual countries, offering government services in all official languages is crucial but often challenging due to the need for human translators.

Implementation: A provincial government, serving a highly diverse population, incorporated ChatGPT to offer real-time translation for its online services. Citizens could input queries in one language and receive responses in another.
Outcome: Accessibility to government services improved significantly, especially for minority language speakers. This led to increased inclusivity and a more engaged citizenry.

5. Crime Reporting and Safety Tips:
Background: Reporting minor crimes or suspicious activities and receiving safety tips is crucial for public safety, but not everyone is comfortable contacting the police directly.
Implementation: A city's police department integrated ChatGPT into its official app. Residents could report non-urgent matters, ask about safety protocols, or even receive guidance on neighborhood watch programs.
Outcome: There was a noticeable increase in public engagement with the police. The system allowed citizens to feel more connected and safer, knowing they had a direct, non-intimidating line of communication with law enforcement.

These examples illuminate the potential of ChatGPT and similar AI models in enhancing public service delivery, making processes efficient, and ensuring an informed and engaged citizenry.

CHAPTER 2: SETTING UP CHATGPT IN GOVERNMENT SYSTEMS

In this chapter, we discuss technical aspects of setting up ChatGPT for use in government systems, such as integration with existing infrastructure, compliance with regulatory standards, data handling procedures, and security considerations.

Successful Deployment and Integration

Introduction:

A successful deployment of ChatGPT starts with understanding the AI model's technical specifications, working principles, and data requirements. This foundational understanding is crucial for effective integration with existing systems and infrastructure.

In practical terms, the integration process involves connecting the AI model with the government's IT infrastructure, including servers, databases, and other software systems. This can be a complex process that may require customization and fine-tuning based on the unique setup of the government's existing systems.

To facilitate this integration, OpenAI provides comprehensive documentation and programming interfaces that developers can use to connect ChatGPT to various software applications. These resources are designed to make the integration process as smooth as possible, but it's important to recognize that some technical expertise is required.
This is why it's crucial to have a skilled technical team involved in the process.

Compliance with Regulatory Standards

A crucial aspect of implementing AI tools like ChatGPT in government systems is compliance with regulatory standards. These standards govern data protection, accessibility, and various other aspects of IT system operation in the public sector. They are designed to ensure that all systems are used ethically, safely, and responsibly.

For instance, if ChatGPT is used to process personal data, it must comply with relevant data protection laws. This might include the General Data Protection Regulation (GDPR) in the European Union or similar regulations in other jurisdictions. These laws stipulate how personal data can be collected, stored, and used, and non-compliance can result in substantial penalties.

In addition, if ChatGPT is used to deliver public services, it must meet certain accessibility standards to ensure that all citizens can use the services effectively. These standards ensure that technology is accessible to people with various disabilities, helping to ensure that the benefits of AI are available to everyone.

Data Handling Procedures

Another key aspect of implementing ChatGPT in government systems is the establishment of data handling procedures. Given the sensitive nature of much of the data held by governments, it's crucial to handle this data ethically and responsibly.

ChatGPT operates on the basis of input and output data. This means it receives data (input), processes it, and then generates a response (output). To protect the privacy of individuals, it's important to ensure that any personal data used in this process is handled appropriately. This might involve anonymizing data before it's input into ChatGPT, using secure channels to transmit data, and securely storing any output data.

Security Measures

Lastly, robust security measures are vital to the successful deployment of ChatGPT. Governments hold a vast amount of sensitive information, making them a prime target for cyber attacks. Therefore, it's critical to ensure that AI tools like ChatGPT are deployed within a secure IT environment.

Security measures might include firewalls, secure servers, data encryption, and strong access controls. Additionally, regular security audits can help identify potential vulnerabilities and ensure that the system is kept updated to protect against new threats.

In conclusion, setting up ChatGPT in government systems involves a mix of technical tasks, regulatory compliance, data handling procedures, and security measures. By taking the time to carefully plan and implement these steps, governments can effectively integrate ChatGPT into their operations, paving the way for improved efficiency and enhanced public service delivery.

Technical Integration: The Core of Implementing ChatGPT

The technical integration of ChatGPT into government systems is a fundamental process that enables the utilization of AI capabilities. Depending on the specific use case, ChatGPT could be integrated with different existing platforms. Let's look deeper into this process.

The types of systems that ChatGPT can be integrated with are vast and include Customer Relationship Management (CRM) systems, Content Management Systems (CMS), database systems, and more. These systems serve different functions within a government entity:

- CRM Systems: These are used to manage a government's interaction with current and potential citizens. They analyze the data about citizens' history, improving business relationships, focusing specifically on citizen retention, and driving sales growth. In this context, ChatGPT can be used to handle a variety of tasks, such as answering common questions, providing detailed information about procedures or laws, or assisting with form filling.

- CMS: Content Management Systems are used to manage the creation and modification of digital content. For governments, this could mean anything from managing the content on government websites to handling digital archives. ChatGPT could be integrated into such systems to assist with content creation, editing, and management.

- Internal Databases: Government entities manage a lot of data. These databases can range from census data to tax records. Depending on the nature of the data and the use case, ChatGPT can be used to extract, summarize, analyze, or process this information.

In order to technically integrate ChatGPT with these existing systems, developers need to use APIs or Application Programming Interfaces. APIs can be thought of as bridges between different software systems, allowing them to communicate and work together. OpenAI provides well-documented APIs for ChatGPT that developers can use for integration.

These APIs allow developers to send inputs (prompts) to ChatGPT and receive outputs (responses) that can then be used in the government system. For instance, in a CRM system, a user's question could be sent as a prompt to the ChatGPT API, and the API would return an output that could then be displayed as the answer to the user's question.

However, a key part of this integration process is the handling of data. Government systems often use a wide variety of data formats and standards. Before integration, it's essential to ensure that data fed into the ChatGPT API is in a format that it can process and that the responses from ChatGPT are in a format that the government system can use. This might involve creating additional code or using data transformation tools.

In conclusion, technical integration is the first essential step to deploy ChatGPT within government systems, and it requires an understanding of both the AI model's working mechanism and the technical aspects of the existing systems. It is a task that involves cooperation between AI experts, software developers, and the government entity, and its successful completion sets the stage for the efficient use of AI in enhancing government operations.

Compatibility and Data Formats: Crucial Aspects of Integration

Integration of ChatGPT into existing government systems requires careful consideration of compatibility issues. These issues could arise from differences in technology stacks, interfaces, but most commonly from differences in data formats.

As a language model, ChatGPT uses text data as input and produces text data as output. The formats and structures of the input and output data are well defined. However, government systems handle a vast variety of data types, including but not limited to structured databases, document-based data, scanned files, or even audio and video files. Therefore, developers must ensure that these data can be transformed into a format that is understandable by ChatGPT.

Data Conversion and Transformation

Data conversion or transformation is a common task in software development and especially important when integrating disparate systems. In the context of ChatGPT, data conversion might be needed to transform the data from the original format used in the government systems into a text-based format that can be used as input to the AI model.

For instance, if a government system uses a database to store information, a conversion process might be needed to transform the structured data in the database into a text-based format. This could involve extracting relevant fields from the database, combining them into sentences or paragraphs, and then sending these text strings as input to ChatGPT.

Similarly, if a government system uses scanned documents as a data source, a process known as Optical Character Recognition (OCR) could be used to convert the images in the scanned documents into text data. Once the text data has been extracted, it can be used as input to ChatGPT.

Output Data Processing

The output from ChatGPT is also in text format, so a conversion process might be needed to transform this data into a format that can be used by the government systems. For instance, if the output from ChatGPT needs to be stored in a database, it might be necessary to parse the text data into separate fields that can be stored in the database. This would involve defining rules or algorithms that can identify the relevant parts of the output text and map them to the appropriate database fields.

In conclusion, compatibility and data conversion are crucial aspects of the technical integration of ChatGPT into government systems. By understanding the data formats used by ChatGPT and the existing systems, and by developing effective data conversion processes, developers can ensure a seamless integration of the AI model. This in turn enables governments to leverage the power of AI to enhance their operations and deliver better services to the public.

Scalability: Planning for Growth

Scalability is a vital aspect of any software system, and it is even more crucial when dealing with AI implementations like ChatGPT. Scalability refers to the system's ability to handle an increasing amount of work or its potential to accommodate growth in the future. When we speak about scalability in the context of integrating ChatGPT into government systems, we refer to both the scalability of the AI model itself and the broader system within which it is deployed.

Scalability of ChatGPT

As a product of OpenAI, ChatGPT is designed to handle a significant number of requests concurrently. OpenAI's infrastructure is cloud-based and highly scalable, meaning it can handle a large number of requests without any noticeable degradation in performance. This ensures that as the number of users or requests increases, ChatGPT itself can scale to meet this demand.

However, to ensure a seamless user experience, developers should consider rate limiting, which is a technique for controlling the amount of incoming and outgoing traffic to or from a network. OpenAI's API documentation provides guidance on how to handle rate limits correctly.

Scalability of the Government Systems

While ChatGPT is designed to be highly scalable, the systems into which it is being integrated also need to be scalable to prevent any bottlenecks. As the use of ChatGPT grows, the volume of data it processes will likely increase.

This could put additional load on databases, network bandwidth, and other system resources. Therefore, the infrastructure that supports these systems needs to be robust and scalable.

This might involve using load balancing strategies, where workloads are distributed across multiple computing resources to ensure no single resource becomes a bottleneck. Alternatively, it might involve using cloud-based systems that can be easily scaled up or down based on demand.

Moreover, government systems are likely to experience peaks in demand at specific times, such as during the tax filing period or when new services or initiatives are launched. These systems should be designed to handle these periods of high demand without compromising on performance or user experience.

Monitoring and Adjusting

Finally, it's essential to monitor system performance continuously and make necessary adjustments to handle increased demand. This might involve adding more server capacity, optimizing database queries, or upgrading network infrastructure. Regular monitoring helps identify potential issues before they become critical and ensures that the system can continue to provide a high-quality service even as demand grows.

In conclusion, scalability should be a key consideration during the integration process. By ensuring that both ChatGPT and the government systems can handle increased demand, governments can ensure a smooth, efficient service that meets the needs of their citizens, regardless of how much those needs grow over time.

Compliance with Regulatory Standards: Ensuring Ethical and Legal AI Use

Artificial intelligence use in public sectors, such as government institutions, is indeed subject to a myriad of regulations. These rules and standards ensure that AI technologies are used responsibly, ethically, and lawfully. When integrating ChatGPT into government systems, these regulations need to be thoroughly understood and followed to avoid legal repercussions and to maintain public trust.

Data Protection Laws

Data protection laws are key regulations that apply to AI use, especially when it involves the processing of personal data. For example, in the European Union, the General Data Protection Regulation (GDPR) provides a comprehensive legal framework for data protection. It outlines principles for data management and rights of individuals, including the right to access their personal data, the right to rectification, the right to erasure, and the right to data portability.

If ChatGPT is used to process personal data of EU citizens, for instance, in a citizen service portal where users may ask personalized questions, the AI application must be designed in a way that complies with GDPR. This could involve measures such as obtaining explicit consent before collecting or processing personal data, providing users with options to view, correct, or delete their data, or ensuring that data is processed in a way that guarantees adequate security.

Accessibility Standards

Accessibility standards are another critical set of regulations that apply to public-facing government services. These standards ensure that all citizens, including those with disabilities, can access and use government services effectively.

In the context of AI, this could mean that any interfaces or platforms that use ChatGPT should be designed in accordance with relevant accessibility guidelines. For instance, in the United States, Section 508 of the Rehabilitation Act requires that all electronic and information technology developed, procured, maintained, or used by the federal government be accessible to people with disabilities.

In practice, this could involve ensuring that any text generated by ChatGPT is compatible with screen readers, providing alternatives for any non-text content, or ensuring that the service can be navigated using only a keyboard. It's also crucial to ensure that the language used by ChatGPT is clear and easy to understand, as this can be a significant barrier to accessibility.

Standards for Public Sector IT Systems

Governments also have specific standards and best practices for their IT systems. These may relate to security, interoperability, or performance, among other things. It's important to ensure that the use of ChatGPT aligns with these standards.

For instance, there may be requirements related to data encryption, user authentication, system uptime, or disaster recovery. The ChatGPT integration should be designed in a way that upholds these standards, either by adhering to them directly or by ensuring that the broader system within which ChatGPT operates adheres to them.

In conclusion, ensuring compliance with regulatory standards is a critical aspect of integrating ChatGPT into government systems. By adhering to these regulations, governments can ensure that they use AI responsibly, ethically, and legally, helping to maintain public trust and avoiding legal complications. It is highly recommended to involve legal and compliance teams from the initial stages of the AI integration project to ensure that all regulatory aspects are covered.

Data Handling Procedures: An Essential Step Towards Privacy and Ethics

The handling of data, especially personal or sensitive information, is a critical aspect of deploying AI models like ChatGPT in government systems. Governments, by virtue of their function, are custodians of vast amounts of personal and sensitive data. The ways in which this data is collected, processed, stored, and disposed of can have significant impacts on privacy, security, and public trust.

When integrating ChatGPT into government systems, it is imperative to establish clear data handling procedures that adhere to the highest standards of data protection and privacy. These procedures should cover the entire data lifecycle - from the moment the data is collected until it is disposed of.

Data Collection and Input

Before any data is inputted into ChatGPT, it should be carefully scrutinized to ensure that it does not contain sensitive or personal information that could be misused or could compromise the privacy of individuals. If personal data needs to be processed, explicit consent should be obtained wherever applicable, in line with data protection regulations.

If possible, data should be anonymized before being inputted into ChatGPT. Anonymization involves removing or replacing identifying details so that it is not possible to link the data back to an individual. This reduces the risk of personal data being inadvertently exposed or misused.

Data Processing and Storage

ChatGPT does not store personal data after the conversation ends, which minimizes the risk of data leakage. However, while an interaction with ChatGPT is ongoing, data is temporarily stored and processed. During this time, it is crucial that the data is adequately protected.

Strong encryption should be applied when data is in transit to prevent interception. The principle of data minimization should be adhered to, meaning that only the minimum necessary amount of data should be processed.

In terms of storage, the architecture of the system should be designed in such a way that sensitive data is isolated and secure. Access to this data should be strictly controlled and logged to ensure accountability.

Data Disposal

After a conversation ends, ChatGPT does not retain the data. However, governments should be aware that any logs or backups of the system could potentially contain remnants of sensitive data. Therefore, data disposal procedures should be implemented to ensure that these remnants are securely deleted when no longer needed.

In conclusion, data handling procedures play a pivotal role in protecting privacy and ensuring the ethical use of AI. Governments should design these procedures with a strong emphasis on data protection and privacy, and regularly review and update them to account for new challenges or changes in the regulatory landscape. This will help ensure that the use of ChatGPT aligns with the highest standards of data protection and privacy, thereby safeguarding the public trust.

Security Considerations: Safeguarding Public Trust and Data Integrity

When it comes to public service operations, cybersecurity is a crucial component. It ensures the protection of sensitive data and public trust. Therefore, when integrating an AI tool like ChatGPT into government systems, it's paramount to put robust cybersecurity measures in place to guard against data breaches and unauthorized access.

Comprehensive Cybersecurity Measures

A comprehensive security system is built on several key components. The government infrastructure must be equipped with the latest firewalls to block unauthorized access. Secure servers should be used to store sensitive information, and data encryption should be employed during transit to prevent interception.

Access controls play a critical role in ensuring only authorized individuals can access sensitive data or the AI system. The principle of least privilege should be implemented, meaning individuals should only be granted the access rights they need to perform their duties, thereby limiting the potential for unauthorized access or misuse.

In addition, multi-factor authentication can provide an additional layer of security. This type of system requires more than one method of authentication from independent categories of credentials, making it harder for unauthorized users to gain access.

Regular Security Audits and System Updates

Conducting regular security audits is a proactive way to identify and rectify potential vulnerabilities in the system. Audits can assess the effectiveness of current security measures, identify weaknesses, and provide recommendations for improvement. They should be carried out by independent, qualified auditors to ensure objectivity and comprehensiveness.

Furthermore, keeping the system updated is a crucial component of cybersecurity. As new threats emerge, updates often include patches for these vulnerabilities. A regular schedule for system updates should be established, and emergency updates should be implemented when critical vulnerabilities are identified.

Disaster Recovery Planning

A disaster recovery plan should be put in place to ensure that services can be quickly restored in the event of a major incident or breach. This involves regular data backups, plans for restoring services, and procedures for investigating and learning from incidents.

In Conclusion

In conclusion, integrating ChatGPT into government systems is a complex process that requires careful planning and execution. This includes not just the technical aspects of the AI integration, but also significant considerations around compliance with regulations, ethical data handling procedures, and rigorous cybersecurity measures.

By adhering to these principles, government institutions can mitigate potential risks and effectively leverage ChatGPT for improving public services. This will pave the

way for a more innovative, efficient, and responsive public sector, ready to meet the demands of the 21st century. In the subsequent chapters, we will explore specific applications of ChatGPT in various areas of government operations.

Examples:

1. Real-time Data Analysis for City Planning:
Background: City planners constantly grapple with massive data sets, from traffic patterns to utility usage, to make informed decisions.
Implementation: A metropolitan city used ChatGPT integrated with its data analysis tools. When a city planner needed insights, they could ask the AI model. For instance, "What were the peak traffic times in the downtown area last month?" ChatGPT, having access to real-time traffic data, would provide an instantaneous response.
Outcome: City planning became more agile. Decisions could be made faster, grounded in real-time data, without planners having to sift through databases manually.

2. Automated Grant Application Review:
Background: Governments often provide grants to startups, non-profits, and research entities. The application review process can be tedious, requiring checking compliance with criteria, prior history, and more.
Implementation: A national funding agency integrated ChatGPT into its grant review process. When an application was submitted, ChatGPT would first review it, checking for compliance with fundamental criteria, analyzing the applicant's history, and even flagging potential areas of concern.

Outcome: The first-level screening process became significantly more efficient, allowing human reviewers to focus on nuanced evaluations instead of basic compliance.

3. AI-driven Legislative History Search:
Background: Understanding legislative history is crucial when drafting new laws or making legal decisions.
Implementation: A legal department within a federal government integrated ChatGPT with its legislative databases. When someone needed to understand the history or context of a particular law, they would ask ChatGPT. For instance, "What discussions led to the amendment of Article X in 2005?" ChatGPT would pull up relevant debate transcripts, amendments, and related documentation.
Outcome: Legal professionals saved hours they would have otherwise spent manually searching through archives, leading to more informed and timely legal decisions.

4. Environment Monitoring and Alert Systems:
Background: Governments are responsible for monitoring environmental factors, from air quality to radiation levels, to ensure public safety.
Implementation: An environmental protection agency, in a region prone to industrial pollution, used ChatGPT integrated with real-time monitoring tools. If sensors detected abnormal levels, ChatGPT would instantly alert relevant officials with specifics and even suggest preliminary actions based on historical data.
Outcome: The region saw quicker response times to environmental anomalies, potentially averting health crises and ensuring swift accountability.

5. Tax Query Resolution System:

Background: Tax codes can be complex, leading to numerous queries from the public, especially around tax season.
Implementation: A national tax agency used ChatGPT as a front-end interface for citizen queries. Instead of navigating complicated manuals, citizens could ask direct questions like, "How do I declare overseas income?" or "What's the deadline for individual tax returns?", and receive clear, instantaneous answers.
Outcome: The agency witnessed a dramatic drop in wait times for query resolutions. Moreover, since ChatGPT could handle a majority of standard questions, human agents were free to address more complex issues.

Each of these examples underscores the versatility and depth of ChatGPT's technical capabilities, especially when integrated with other systems, and how they can be harnessed to improve government functions.

CHAPTER 3: PRIVACY, SECURITY, AND ETHICAL CONSIDERATIONS

This chapter delves deeper into the ethical and security implications of AI use in government. We cover principles of responsible AI usage, ensuring user privacy, anonymizing and handling sensitive data, dealing with AI bias, and promoting transparency in AI systems.

The rapid rise of AI technologies and their adoption in various sectors has brought transformative changes, the public sector being no exception. AI-powered systems like ChatGPT present enormous potential for augmenting public sector operations. They can streamline administrative processes, boost productivity, inform policy-making, and vastly improve public service delivery. However, these revolutionary capabilities come with a host of challenges and concerns revolving around privacy, security, and ethical matters. It's crucial to thoroughly address these issues to ensure a responsible and ethical utilization of AI in government.

Understanding the Implications of AI

While the potential of AI for public sector operations is tremendous, it is not without its complexities. AI technologies, by their very nature, involve processing large amounts of data, some of which can be highly sensitive, especially when it comes to governmental use. Privacy concerns arise, as mishandling such data can lead to serious violations of individual rights and legal repercussions. Security becomes a paramount concern, as these systems, if not adequately protected, can become targets for malicious attacks aiming to compromise the data.

Moreover, ethical considerations come into play. AI systems, including ChatGPT, are tools that can replicate or even magnify societal biases present in their training data. Unchecked, these systems could potentially lead to unfair or discriminatory outcomes in public services, exacerbating social inequality rather than mitigating it.

Navigating the Challenges: Responsible AI in Government

Addressing these concerns requires an approach grounded in the principles of responsible AI use. These principles guide the deployment and application of AI technologies in a way that upholds the core values of fairness, privacy, security, transparency, and accountability.

Government entities must take active steps to minimize and manage the risks associated with AI use. They must put in place robust privacy policies, secure data handling practices, and rigorous security protocols. Furthermore, they need to ensure that the AI systems they employ are transparent in their operation and accountable for their outputs. Mechanisms for regular audits, monitoring for biases, and rectification of any discriminatory practices should be an integral part of any AI deployment strategy in government.

This chapter serves as a roadmap to navigate these complex issues, providing an overview of the challenges and the best practices for mitigating them. By exploring the concepts of privacy, security, and ethics in the context of AI in government, this chapter offers a comprehensive framework for responsible AI use, enabling government entities to harness the benefits of AI technologies like ChatGPT while minimizing potential risks.

Responsible AI is an umbrella term that encompasses the ethical, transparent, and accountable use of AI

technologies. It goes beyond merely employing AI for efficiency or productivity, focusing on a holistic approach that considers societal and individual impacts, privacy concerns, and security issues. To ensure responsible use of AI like ChatGPT in government, the following principles should be carefully adhered to:

1. **Fairness:**

AI systems should be designed and used in a way that promotes fairness and prevents bias. This involves making sure that the AI does not favor one group over another or discriminate based on factors such as race, gender, age, or socio-economic status. For example, if ChatGPT is used in a public-facing role, it should treat all users equally, irrespective of their demographics or personal characteristics.

2. **Transparency:**

Transparency refers to the openness of an AI system's functioning. It means that users should be able to understand how the AI works, what data it uses, and how it makes decisions. Transparency can be challenging to achieve, especially with complex AI models like ChatGPT, but it's crucial for building trust with users and stakeholders.

3. **Accountability:**

Accountability in AI usage refers to the need for systems to be overseen by humans who can understand their operation and take responsibility for their outcomes. This

principle necessitates regular monitoring and auditing of AI systems to ensure they are working as intended and to identify and rectify any issues promptly.

4. Privacy:

The use of AI should respect and protect the privacy of individuals. This is particularly important in the government sector, which often handles sensitive data. Any data used to train or interact with AI systems like ChatGPT should be anonymized and handled in line with robust data protection standards.

5. Security:

AI systems can be vulnerable to attacks and misuse, making security a key principle of responsible AI usage. This involves safeguarding systems from unauthorized access, ensuring data encryption, and maintaining up-to-date protections against cybersecurity threats.
Adhering to these principles not only helps governments avoid potential pitfalls and risks associated with AI use but also helps ensure that these technologies are used for the betterment of public services and the broader society. In the following sections, we will delve deeper into each of these principles, exploring practical measures that can be taken to uphold them.

Fairness is a cornerstone principle in responsible AI usage. As AI models learn from the data they are trained on, they can inadvertently acquire and perpetuate biases present in that data. This potential for bias in AI has significant implications for government use, where equitable treatment and fairness are paramount. When ChatGPT or any AI system is used in public service delivery or policy-making, it's critical to ensure that it doesn't contribute to or exacerbate existing inequities.

Understanding Bias in AI

Bias in AI can occur due to several reasons. Firstly, it can stem from biased training data. If the data used to train the AI system contains biases, the system can learn and replicate these biases in its operations. For instance, if the training data over-represents a particular demographic group, the AI model might perform better for that group, resulting in biased outcomes.

Secondly, bias can occur due to biased problem formulation or algorithmic design. If the design of the AI system inherently favors certain outcomes or groups over others, it can lead to bias.

Finally, bias can arise from the misuse or inappropriate application of AI tools. If an AI model developed for one context is used inappropriately in a different context without necessary adjustments, it can lead to biased results.

Minimizing Bias and Ensuring Fairness

To ensure fairness in AI usage, governments must take active steps to minimize bias. This involves several stages, from data collection and training to deployment and monitoring.

Data Collection and Training: **Governments should ensure that the data used to train AI systems is representative of the diverse population they serve. This involves careful data collection strategies that avoid over or under-representation of certain groups. Furthermore, during model training, techniques like fairness constraints, adversarial de-biasing, and re-sampling can be used to minimize bias.**

Deployment: **When deploying AI systems, governments should ensure that they are used appropriately and in contexts that they were designed for. The performance of the AI system should be tested across diverse groups to ensure it performs equitably.**

Monitoring and Auditing: **Regular monitoring and auditing of AI systems are necessary to check for any biased outcomes. This involves tracking the system's performance over time and across different demographic groups. If biases are identified, the system should be adjusted or retrained to correct them.**

In conclusion, ensuring fairness in AI is not a one-time effort but a continuous process that requires active and ongoing commitment. It is a critical component of responsible AI usage, especially in the public sector, where equitable service and policy are of utmost importance.

Transparency is a key principle in the responsible use of AI technologies like ChatGPT. The goal of transparency is to make the operation and decision-making processes of AI understandable to users and stakeholders, which is essential for building trust and ensuring accountability.

Understanding the Importance of Transparency

Transparency in AI usage is crucial for several reasons. It helps users understand what the AI can and can't do, which is essential for setting appropriate expectations. It allows stakeholders to evaluate the AI system's decisions, which is necessary for accountability and oversight. Furthermore, it enables affected individuals to comprehend how decisions that impact them are made, which is a basic requirement for fairness and due process.

Achieving Transparency in AI

Achieving transparency in AI can be challenging, especially given the complexity of models like ChatGPT. However, several strategies can be employed to enhance transparency in AI usage:

Clear Documentation: Comprehensive documentation is a crucial first step towards achieving transparency. This should include information on how the AI system works, what data it uses, its capabilities and limitations, and the logic or rules it uses to make decisions. It should be written in a manner that is understandable to non-technical users.

Explainability: In addition to documenting how the AI system works in general, it's also important to provide explanations for specific outcomes or decisions generated by the AI. These explanations should help users understand why the AI system made a particular decision. Techniques such as Local Interpretable Model-Agnostic

Explanations (LIME) or SHapley Additive exPlanations (SHAP) can be employed to generate these explanations.

User Interface Design: The design of the user interface can also contribute to transparency. It should clearly communicate what the AI is doing at any given time, provide feedback on user input, and present AI-generated outcomes in an understandable manner.

Transparency in Data Handling: Transparent data handling practices are also important. Users should be informed about what data the AI system collects, how it uses this data, and how it protects privacy and security.

Engagement with Stakeholders: Finally, engaging with stakeholders can enhance transparency. Regular meetings, consultations, and reviews can provide opportunities for stakeholders to ask questions, raise concerns, and learn more about the AI system.

In conclusion, while achieving transparency in AI can be challenging, it is a necessary part of responsible AI usage. By employing strategies like clear documentation, explainability, thoughtful user interface design, transparent data handling practices, and stakeholder engagement, governments can make the operation and decision-making processes of AI systems more understandable and trustworthy.

Accountability is a vital principle for ensuring that AI systems like ChatGPT are used responsibly. It refers to the idea that entities (including governments) using AI systems must take responsibility for the decisions these systems make and the impacts they have. This responsibility extends to the development, deployment, and monitoring stages of AI system usage.

Why Accountability Matters in AI Usage

Accountability is essential for several reasons:

1. Responsibility for Actions: When an AI system makes a decision or takes an action, there needs to be a clear line of responsibility. This is particularly important when the AI's actions have significant consequences, such as influencing policy decisions or citizen services.

2. Trust Building: Accountability mechanisms can help build trust between the AI system, its users, and those affected by its actions. People are more likely to trust an AI system if they know there is an entity responsible for its actions and that this entity can be held to account.

3. Remedying Mistakes: Accountability also ensures that there are mechanisms in place to correct errors. AI systems, despite their advanced capabilities, can still make mistakes. An accountable entity can take responsibility for these errors and take steps to remedy them.

How to Ensure Accountability in AI Usage

Ensuring accountability in AI usage involves multiple strategies:

Clear Responsibility Structures: **The responsibility for an AI system's decisions and actions should be clearly defined. This includes responsibility for developing and deploying the AI system, as well as responsibility for monitoring its use and addressing any issues that arise.**

Audit Trails: **Audit trails that record the decisions made by the AI system can be valuable tools for ensuring accountability. These trails can be reviewed to understand how the AI system made a decision, identify any errors or biases, and determine how to correct them.**

Oversight Mechanisms: **Oversight mechanisms, such as internal review boards or third-party audits, can provide additional layers of accountability. These mechanisms can independently evaluate the AI system's performance, assess compliance with ethical and legal standards, and make recommendations for improvement.**

Redress Mechanisms: **Redress mechanisms allow users or those affected by an AI system's actions to challenge these actions. This could be in the form of a complaint system, an appeals process, or some other method of voicing concerns and seeking redress.**

In conclusion, accountability is a key principle for responsible AI usage. By implementing clear responsibility structures, audit trails, oversight mechanisms, and redress mechanisms, governments can ensure that they are accountable for the actions of AI systems like ChatGPT.

Privacy and security are paramount considerations in AI use, especially within the context of government operations which often deal with sensitive and personal data.

Privacy in AI Usage

Privacy refers to the right of individuals to control how their personal information is collected and used. AI systems, particularly language models like ChatGPT, have the capability to process vast amounts of data, some of which could be personal. Therefore, it's critical to have measures in place to protect user privacy.

There are several strategies for ensuring privacy in AI usage:

Data Minimization: Only collect the minimum data necessary for the AI to perform its function. This reduces the risk of unnecessary data being mishandled or misused.
Anonymization: Wherever possible, data should be anonymized so it cannot be linked back to individuals. This includes removing identifiable information and using techniques like data obfuscation or aggregation.

Consent and Transparency: Users should be informed about what data is being collected, how it's being used, and who it's being shared with. Wherever possible, explicit consent should be obtained for data collection and use.

Security in AI Usage

Security in AI usage pertains to the measures taken to protect data from unauthorized access, alteration, disclosure, or destruction. AI systems, due to their digital nature, can be vulnerable to cyberattacks, making security measures essential. Here are some key strategies for ensuring security:

Data Encryption: Encrypting data transforms it into a code that can only be accessed with a decryption key. Data should be encrypted both when it's stored (at rest) and when it's sent over a network (in transit).

Access Controls: These determine who has the ability to access data. Robust access controls can prevent unauthorized users from accessing sensitive data.
Regular Audits and Updates: Regular security audits can help identify potential vulnerabilities in the system, while regular updates can ensure the system is protected against new threats.

Incident Response Plan: This is a plan for how to respond in the event of a security breach. It can help minimize the damage and ensure a swift return to normal operations.

In conclusion, privacy and security are critical aspects of responsible AI usage. By adhering to best practices in data minimization, anonymization, consent, transparency, encryption, access control, audits, and incident response, governments can ensure the AI systems they use are both privacy-preserving and secure.

Indeed, ensuring user privacy is a cornerstone of responsible AI use, especially in the context of government. Here is a deeper exploration of these strategies:

Data Minimization: The principle of data minimization involves limiting data collection and processing to what is directly relevant and necessary to accomplish a specified purpose. In the context of using AI like ChatGPT in government services, this might mean that only the specific information needed to provide a service or make a decision should be processed, while other unrelated personal data should be left out of the AI's scope. This not only helps to maintain user privacy but also reduces the risk of potential data misuse or exposure.

Anonymization: Anonymization refers to the process of removing personally identifiable information from data sets, so that the individuals whom the data describe remain anonymous. This process can be a valuable method of protecting individual privacy, particularly when dealing with large data sets. Techniques can include removing direct identifiers, such as names and social security numbers, as well as secondary identifiers, such as postcodes or unique characteristics, that could be used to infer an individual's identity.

Consent: Consent is a critical element of data privacy and a fundamental principle of many data protection laws, including the General Data Protection Regulation (GDPR). Before collecting or processing personal data, government entities should obtain explicit, informed consent from the individual. This means providing clear information about what data will be collected, why it is needed, how it will be used and stored, and who will have access to it.

Security Measures: Robust security measures are essential to protecting data privacy. This can include physical security measures (like secured data centers), technical measures (like firewalls, encryption, and secure network protocols), and administrative measures (like policies and procedures that guide safe data handling practices).

Regular audits and assessments can help to ensure these security measures remain effective and up-to-date.

In summary, by taking a proactive and comprehensive approach to user privacy, governments can effectively balance the innovative capabilities of AI tools like ChatGPT with the need to protect individual privacy. This not only fosters trust among users but also helps to uphold the principles of fairness, transparency, and respect that underpin all government operations.

Indeed, handling sensitive data is a critical concern, particularly in the context of government operations where sensitive information could include personally identifiable information (PII), financial data, health records, or classified state information. Here are some key considerations:

Data Collection: The process of gathering data should be performed carefully, with clear intentions and scope. Governments should ensure that data is collected from legitimate and secure sources, and that data collection practices align with local and international regulations. Any sensitive information that is not necessary for the task at hand should be avoided.

Data Processing: This refers to how data is analyzed, transferred, or otherwise used after collection. Sensitive data should be handled with care during these processes. This includes ensuring that data is only accessible to authorized personnel, that it's used strictly for its intended purpose, and that all data processing activities are compliant with relevant regulations.

Data Storage: Storing sensitive data safely is of paramount importance. Various security measures such as firewalls, secure servers, and strong access controls should be in place. Moreover, sensitive data should be encrypted, both when at rest and in transit. Encryption converts data into a code, preventing unauthorized access.

Data Anonymization: As previously discussed, anonymization is the process of removing identifying attributes from data, rendering it impossible (or at least extremely difficult) to link the data back to the individual it pertains to. Techniques include aggregation (where individual data points are combined into groups), pseudonymization (replacing identifiers with pseudonyms), and data masking (concealing certain data fields).

Data Disposal: Lastly, once the data is no longer required, it must be disposed of securely. This can involve permanently deleting electronic files, ensuring outdated physical records are properly destroyed, and that old storage devices are wiped clean. It's important to confirm that once data is erased, it cannot be recovered.

In summary, responsible handling of sensitive data is vital for maintaining trust and ensuring ethical AI use in government. Rigorous data handling procedures that encompass collection, processing, storage, and disposal are key to protecting user privacy and ensuring regulatory compliance. The application of AI in government brings enormous potential, but it must be accompanied by an equivalent commitment to ethical data practices.

Dealing with AI bias effectively requires a multifaceted approach, spanning the lifecycle of AI deployment from design to monitoring. Here's how:

Bias in Training Data: Since AI systems like ChatGPT learn from data, any biases in the training data can be learned and replicated by the AI. For example, if the training data contains stereotyped or prejudiced language, the AI could reproduce these biases in its responses. Similarly, if the data underrepresents certain demographic groups, the AI may not perform as well for those groups. Thus, it's crucial to carefully curate and review the training data to ensure it is comprehensive and fair.

Bias in Model Design: Even with unbiased data, biases can emerge in how an AI interprets that data. This can occur if the model is overly simplistic, failing to capture the complexities of real-world phenomena, or if it overweights certain features. To mitigate this, model design should involve diverse teams and perspectives to counteract potential blind spots. Moreover, using a variety of AI models and techniques can help to ensure robustness.

Testing and Auditing: Regular testing and auditing of AI systems can help to identify and correct biases. Tests should be designed to uncover both obvious and subtle biases and should be performed under a range of different conditions. Audits should also be conducted periodically by independent third parties to ensure impartiality.

Feedback Mechanisms: Finally, implementing feedback mechanisms allows users to report suspected biases. This can provide valuable real-world insights that may not be captured by testing or auditing.

In conclusion, dealing with AI bias is not a one-time task but an ongoing process that requires vigilance and commitment. By combining diverse and representative data, robust model design, comprehensive testing and auditing, and user feedback, governments can go a long way towards ensuring fair and equitable AI systems.

Promoting transparency in AI systems involves a number of key steps:

Clear Communication: Information about AI systems and their use should be clearly communicated to the public. This includes how the systems operate, the data they use, the safeguards in place, and the benefits they provide. The language used should be accessible and understandable, free from jargon and technical terms as much as possible.

Explainability: AI outcomes should be explainable. While the underlying algorithms of AI like ChatGPT may be complex, efforts should be made to explain in simple terms how the AI arrived at a particular decision or outcome. This can involve providing information about the type of data the AI uses, the factors it considers, and the logic it applies.

Decision Rights: Even as AI systems take on more responsibilities, it should always be clear that ultimate decision rights rest with humans. AI can support decision-making, but it should not replace human judgment, especially in critical areas like law enforcement or social services.

Openness to Scrutiny: Transparency also involves openness to external scrutiny. This can include independent audits of AI systems, public consultations on AI use, and mechanisms for users to provide feedback or raise concerns.

Promoting transparency in AI systems is crucial for maintaining public trust and ensuring responsible use of AI. It allows for accountability, empowers users, and fosters a culture of open dialogue around AI. By incorporating these strategies, governments can build AI systems that are not only powerful and efficient, but also trusted and understood by the people they serve.

As governments embrace AI technologies like ChatGPT, it is imperative to ensure that these tools are deployed responsibly, respecting individual privacy, ensuring data security, and adhering to a high standard of ethical practice. These technologies, after all, are not simply tools; they are extensions of public service, and they should be held to the same standards and values that guide government operations.

Responsible AI is not just about adhering to rules and regulations; it's about committing to an AI governance model that respects human dignity, values, and rights. This commitment manifests itself through fairness, transparency, accountability, and maintaining privacy and security. AI systems should not only produce effective and efficient outcomes but also ethical and fair ones. Fairness ensures that the AI does not discriminate or produce biased outcomes. Transparency and accountability, on the other hand, ensure that the AI's operations are understandable and explainable, and that there are clear lines of responsibility for its actions.

User privacy is paramount. Governments must take stringent measures to ensure that AI tools respect the privacy of individuals and handle their data with utmost care. This includes minimizing data collection, anonymizing data wherever possible, obtaining consent before processing personal data, and implementing strong cybersecurity measures. These steps are crucial not only for adhering to legal regulations but also for maintaining public trust.

Anonymizing and handling sensitive data with care is a critical aspect of deploying AI in government. All stages of data handling—collection, processing, storage, and disposal—must be handled with care. Special emphasis should be placed on anonymizing data and using encryption to protect data during transit and storage. Dealing with AI bias is another important aspect. AI, if not managed well, can perpetuate or even amplify existing biases. Therefore, regular audits should be conducted to check for any signs of bias and corrective action taken immediately when biases are identified.

Finally, promoting transparency in AI systems is essential to maintain public trust. Governments need to be open about how they use AI and how these systems operate. They should provide clear explanations to users and the public about how decisions are made by these AI systems.

In the following chapters, we'll discuss specific applications of AI in government and how these principles and measures can be applied to ensure responsible and effective use. As we navigate through these applications, remember that the ultimate goal of using AI in government is to improve public service delivery, create value for citizens, and enhance the overall quality of governance.

EXAMPLES:

1. Bias Detection and Correction:
Background: A local government initiated a ChatGPT-based tool for citizens to report neighborhood issues. However, concerns arose that the system might exhibit biases based on the data it was trained on.
Implementation: The government, working with AI ethicists, integrated a bias detection algorithm. Whenever ChatGPT produced an output, this algorithm would cross-check for potential biases. If detected, the system would not only correct the bias but also log it for further analysis.
Outcome: Trust in the ChatGPT reporting system increased as citizens felt their concerns were addressed equitably.

The logged biases also provided a feedback loop to refine the system.

2. Privacy Safeguards in Medical Consultations:
***Background*: A state health department employed ChatGPT for initial medical consultations. Given the sensitive nature of health data, the challenge was to ensure patient confidentiality.**
***Implementation*: Before interacting with ChatGPT, users were informed that no personal identifiers should be shared. ChatGPT was also designed to automatically redact or avoid storing any personal data shared mistakenly. Periodic audits ensured that data handling remained compliant with privacy laws.**
***Outcome*: Patients enjoyed the convenience of immediate consultations without fearing breaches of their personal health information.**

3. Transparency in Decision-Making:
***Background*: A city's traffic department used ChatGPT to analyze traffic patterns and suggest roadwork or modifications. However, residents wanted clarity on how decisions were made.**
***Implementation*: To ensure transparency, the traffic department implemented a feature wherein, for every suggestion made by ChatGPT, an accessible summary of the reasoning was also provided. If ChatGPT suggested a new traffic light at an intersection, it would also list reasons, like "increased pedestrian traffic" or "recent accidents."**
***Outcome*: Residents felt more involved in city decisions and were more understanding of disruptions caused by roadworks.**

4. Avoiding Over-reliance:

***Background*: A national disaster management agency utilized ChatGPT for predictive analyses of disaster-prone areas. While the predictions were accurate most times, there were concerns about solely relying on AI.**

***Implementation*: The agency implemented a "dual-check" system. Predictions from ChatGPT would always be cross-verified by a team of human experts before any action was taken. This ensured that human judgment and intuition supplemented AI predictions.**

***Outcome*: The combined AI-human approach led to more comprehensive disaster predictions, combining the vast data-processing power of ChatGPT with the nuanced understanding of human experts.**

5. Control Over AI-generated Content:

***Background*: A government's public relations department utilized ChatGPT for drafting public statements. However, given the potential for misinformation or content that doesn't align with official stances, controls were essential.**

***Implementation*: Every statement generated by ChatGPT underwent a two-step verification process. First, a sentiment analysis tool would gauge the statement's tone and content. Then, human PR experts would review and approve or modify the statement.**

***Outcome*: The PR department could swiftly generate statements while ensuring that every public communication upheld the standards and ethos of the government.**

These examples emphasize the importance of ethical considerations when deploying ChatGPT in a government

setting. By proactively addressing potential challenges, governments can responsibly leverage the power of AI for public benefit.

CHAPTER 4: CHATGPT FOR INTERNAL COMMUNICATIONS

Explore the various ways in which ChatGPT can be leveraged for internal government communications, such as minute-taking, drafting correspondence, facilitating brainstorming sessions, and training government personnel.

Effective, efficient, and fluid internal communication is the bedrock of any functioning government agency. It allows for coordination between departments, facilitates decision-making, and ensures that every member of the organization is aligned towards its objectives. Historically, achieving this has required significant human effort and resources. However, the advent of artificial intelligence, particularly AI models like ChatGPT, offers an exciting avenue to revolutionize communication practices within the government sector.

Incorporating AI in Internal Communication

The application of AI in the sphere of internal communication could serve as a potent catalyst in enhancing public service and achieving organizational goals. By leveraging AI's capabilities in data processing and language understanding, government agencies can streamline and automate various aspects of internal communications, leading to a significant increase in operational efficiency and employee productivity.

Minute-taking with ChatGPT

One area that stands to benefit greatly from AI's introduction is minute-taking. Meetings are an integral part of government operations, serving as venues for crucial decision-making and strategy formulation. Accurate minutes of these meetings are vital as they serve as official records of decisions made and actions to be taken. Traditionally, this is a manual process and can be prone to human error.

By leveraging ChatGPT, the process of minute-taking can be made more efficient and accurate. The AI model can be programmed to listen in on meetings, transcribing speech into text in real-time. It can identify key points and action items, summarizing them for quick reference later. This not only ensures comprehensive and accurate meeting records but also allows all participants to engage fully without worrying about note-taking.

Drafting Correspondence with ChatGPT

Another area where ChatGPT can be invaluable is in drafting correspondence. Government agencies produce vast amounts of written communication, from internal memos to external communications. The creation of these documents can be time-consuming, particularly given the formal tone and specific language often required. ChatGPT, trained on diverse and extensive text data, can automate the process of drafting these documents. Based on a few key inputs, the model can generate a draft that conforms to the required tone and style. This draft can then be reviewed and edited as necessary by staff members. This not only saves time but also allows personnel to focus their efforts on more complex tasks.

Facilitating Brainstorming Sessions with ChatGPT

Innovation is as crucial in government as it is in any other sector. Brainstorming sessions are common practice in organizations to spur creative thinking and problem-solving. Here, too, ChatGPT can play a role. By providing diverse perspectives based on its training data, ChatGPT can help stimulate new ideas and facilitate more fruitful discussions. However, it's important to note that human oversight and judgement are crucial in assessing and implementing these ideas.

ChatGPT in Training Government Personnel

Finally, the application of ChatGPT extends to training and education within government agencies. The AI model can serve as an interactive tutor, providing instant responses to queries and helping staff learn at their own pace. It can be used to create dynamic training modules, making learning more engaging and effective.

In conclusion, by integrating AI technologies like ChatGPT, government agencies can significantly enhance their internal communication processes. From taking meeting minutes to drafting correspondence, facilitating brainstorming sessions, and training staff, ChatGPT offers a multitude of benefits. However, these advantages must be balanced with responsible and ethical use, ensuring that the use of AI respects privacy, maintains data security, and enhances rather than diminishes the quality of government communication.

Minute-taking is an essential administrative task across all government agencies, serving as the backbone of effective meeting management and organizational record-keeping. It involves the detailed and accurate documentation of proceedings, decisions, and action points that transpire in meetings. Traditionally, this role falls on a dedicated person who must pay careful attention to discussions, sift through various points of view, and translate these into comprehensive, coherent records. This task, though integral, can be time-consuming, subject to human error, and may detract from full participation by the assigned individual.

However, the advent of AI models like ChatGPT has opened up new possibilities for enhancing and streamlining this process. With its advanced language comprehension and generation capabilities, ChatGPT can serve as an automated minute-taker, transcribing speech into text in real-time. This allows for the immediate creation of a detailed record of the meeting, eliminating the need for later transcription and reducing potential inaccuracies associated with memory or interpretation lapses.

Additionally, ChatGPT's capability extends beyond simple transcription. With the ability to understand context and extract key information from a large volume of text, ChatGPT can be programmed to focus on and highlight action items, decisions made, and critical points of discussion during the meeting. This feature can significantly reduce the time and effort required for participants to review the minutes, allowing for immediate clarification, confirmation, or action following the meeting.

With AI-powered minute-taking, every participant can fully engage in the discussions without the burden of keeping detailed records. It also minimizes the risk of miscommunication or missed information, resulting in more effective and efficient meetings. It's important to note, however, that these AI-generated minutes should always be reviewed by human staff to ensure accuracy and context accuracy.

Security and privacy are paramount in this process. When using ChatGPT for minute-taking, it's essential to ensure that the platform is secure and that the data being processed is protected. As discussed in previous chapters, adherence to data handling procedures and regulatory compliance, including data anonymization where possible, is crucial.

In conclusion, leveraging ChatGPT for minute-taking in government settings can offer considerable benefits in terms of efficiency, accuracy, and participant engagement. However, it's essential to balance these advantages with responsible use, ensuring that all activities respect data security and privacy while maintaining the quality and reliability of official meeting records.

Government agencies are involved in a constant flow of written communication, from internal memos, emails, and policy documents to external correspondence with stakeholders, constituents, and other agencies. The creation of these written materials can be a significant administrative burden, consuming valuable time and resources that could be better invested in strategic or high-level tasks.

The drafting process often involves standard formats, repeated language, and common themes, making it an ideal candidate for automation with AI. As an advanced language model, ChatGPT can be leveraged to automate aspects of this drafting process, reducing the administrative load and enabling a more efficient allocation of resources.

ChatGPT can generate draft documents based on provided inputs or prompts. For example, a user could specify the type of document, the intended recipient, the key message, and any other relevant information. ChatGPT can then generate a draft document in line with these instructions, significantly reducing the time and effort required to produce the document.

The generated drafts can then be reviewed, edited, and finalized by staff members, ensuring the final output maintains the necessary human touch, including context-specific nuances, empathy, and cultural awareness. This not only improves the efficiency of the drafting process but also allows government personnel to focus on higher-level tasks that require human judgment and expertise, such as strategic planning, policy development, and stakeholder engagement.

Moreover, ChatGPT can be trained to adhere to the specific writing style and conventions of a particular agency or department, ensuring consistency across all written communications. It can also handle multiple languages, aiding in communication with diverse groups of stakeholders and constituents.

However, as with any application of AI in government, using ChatGPT for drafting correspondence needs to be approached with careful consideration of privacy and security. All data used should be anonymized and handled in compliance with relevant regulations. Additionally, outputs should always be reviewed by a human to ensure they are appropriate, accurate, and align with the government agency's communication policies and standards.

In conclusion, leveraging ChatGPT for drafting correspondence can result in significant time and resource savings for government agencies, while allowing for more focus on complex, strategic tasks. However, it is essential that the implementation of such technology is carried out ethically, transparently, and in compliance with all relevant regulations and standards.

Brainstorming sessions are vital for fostering innovation, generating new ideas, and finding solutions to complex problems within government agencies. These sessions often involve a diverse group of individuals coming together to share perspectives and ideas. However, the ideation process can sometimes stagnate, and this is where AI models like ChatGPT can play a transformative role.

ChatGPT, with its broad training on diverse sources, can act as a facilitator or participant in brainstorming sessions. The model can be prompted with a problem or question and generate a variety of responses based on its training data. This can trigger innovative thinking by offering new perspectives and approaches that may not have been considered. For example, it could provide examples of how similar problems have been addressed in different contexts or generate novel solutions based on its understanding of the problem.

One of the advantages of using ChatGPT in this context is its ability to generate a large number of ideas rapidly. This 'quantity' approach is often beneficial in the early stages of brainstorming, where the aim is to generate as many ideas as possible before narrowing down to the most promising options.

Additionally, using AI in brainstorming sessions can help eliminate potential bias or hierarchy in idea generation, as the AI does not have personal prejudices or vested interests. This can lead to a more inclusive and democratic ideation process.

However, while AI can contribute significantly to brainstorming sessions, it's important to underscore the role of human judgement and expertise. Although ChatGPT can produce novel ideas and suggestions, the feasibility, appropriateness, and ethical implications of these ideas need to be evaluated by human experts. AI can aid the brainstorming process, but ultimately, the decision-making should remain a human endeavor.

Moreover, it's crucial to ensure that using AI in this context adheres to privacy and security standards. For instance, brainstorming sessions might involve sensitive information, and this should be carefully managed to ensure it does not compromise privacy or confidentiality.

In conclusion, ChatGPT can be a powerful tool to facilitate brainstorming sessions within government agencies, stimulating innovative thinking, and providing diverse perspectives. However, its use should be complemented by robust human judgement and adherence to privacy and security standards.

AI models like ChatGPT hold significant potential for enhancing training and education within government agencies. They can transform traditional, often static, training methods into dynamic, interactive learning experiences. This not only leads to more engaging training sessions, but also allows for personalized learning experiences, catering to the unique needs of each individual.

Interactive Training Materials: One of the ways ChatGPT can be utilized is in the creation of interactive training materials. Traditional training materials such as manuals or guides, while informative, can often be monotonous and lack interactivity.

However, with ChatGPT, these materials can be transformed into dynamic learning resources. For instance, ChatGPT can be used to generate scenario-based learning activities. These activities can simulate real-world situations, allowing trainees to apply their knowledge in a safe environment. This approach has been found to increase understanding and retention of information.

Furthermore, interactive quizzes or assessments can be developed using ChatGPT. These can provide immediate feedback to the trainees, helping them to understand their progress and identify areas for improvement.

Virtual Tutor: ChatGPT can also serve as a virtual tutor, available 24/7 to answer queries from trainees. The AI model can answer a wide range of questions, providing explanations, examples, and further resources. This allows trainees to learn at their own pace and get immediate responses to their questions, making learning more efficient.

Using AI for training can also provide valuable data insights. For instance, by analyzing the interactions between ChatGPT and the trainees, trainers can identify common areas of confusion or frequently asked questions. This information can be used to improve the training program and address gaps in knowledge.

While ChatGPT can be a powerful tool for training, it's important to remember that it is not a substitute for human trainers. The AI model can provide information and answer questions, but it doesn't have the contextual understanding or emotional intelligence of a human trainer. Therefore, while ChatGPT can be an effective tool for facilitating learning, it should be used as a complement to, not a replacement for, traditional training methods.

In conclusion, ChatGPT can revolutionize the way training is conducted within government agencies. By developing interactive training materials and acting as a virtual tutor, it can make learning more engaging, personalized, and efficient. However, to harness its full potential, its use should be guided by sound pedagogical principles and supplemented by human-led training.

The potential of AI technologies, such as ChatGPT, to enhance and transform internal communications within government agencies is immense. By automating tasks such as minute-taking and drafting correspondence, facilitating brainstorming sessions and training, ChatGPT can lead to significant efficiency gains, freeing up staff to concentrate on more complex, high-value tasks that require their unique human skills and expertise.

Automation of Repetitive Tasks: The ability of ChatGPT to take over repetitive, time-consuming tasks such as transcribing meetings and drafting routine correspondence can significantly improve operational efficiency. By doing so, government employees are allowed more time to concentrate on the core aspects of their jobs, enhancing productivity and the quality of service delivery to the public.

Facilitation of Innovation: The use of ChatGPT in brainstorming sessions opens up new possibilities for innovative thinking. By offering new ideas or perspectives, it can spark creative problem-solving approaches, driving innovation within government agencies.

Enhancing Training: Through its application in the development of interactive training materials and serving as a virtual tutor, ChatGPT can significantly enhance the training and professional development of government personnel. It allows for personalized, engaging, and effective learning experiences, ultimately contributing to the growth and development of a skilled public service workforce.

However, as we embrace these exciting possibilities, it's equally important to proceed with caution, ensuring the responsible and ethical use of AI. The use of AI in internal communications must always respect and protect the privacy of the users and the data involved. Any information generated by ChatGPT must meet the same standards of quality, accuracy, and professionalism expected of human-generated communications. The deployment of ChatGPT and similar AI tools must be done transparently, with clear communication to all stakeholders about their use, capabilities, and limitations.

In essence, while ChatGPT offers exciting opportunities to revolutionize internal communications within government agencies, its deployment must always align with the principles of responsible AI use. When used ethically and responsibly, AI can play a pivotal role in modernizing government operations, enhancing efficiency, and ultimately, improving the delivery of public services.

EXAMPLES:

1. Integration into Customer Service for Public Utilities:
Background: The city's water department received numerous daily queries regarding billing, service disruptions, and conservation tips.
Implementation: To streamline the process, the department integrated ChatGPT into its website and mobile app. The model was trained on a database of common queries, past resolutions, and city-specific water regulations. For complex issues beyond the AI's capability, the system was designed to seamlessly transfer the query to a human representative.
Outcome: Wait times for query resolutions decreased significantly. Citizens appreciated the instant responses,

and the department was able to allocate human resources to more complex, non-routine tasks.

2. Assisting in Legal Document Analysis:
Background: The state's legal department was often inundated with the task of reviewing large volumes of legal documents to extract relevant information.
Implementation: ChatGPT was trained on a corpus of legal texts and integrated into the department's document management system. Staff could input specific queries, and ChatGPT would rapidly analyze documents, highlighting relevant sections and providing summaries.
Outcome: The time taken for document review was reduced by over 60%. Legal professionals in the department were able to focus on strategy and case building, rather than manual document analysis.

3. Public Engagement and Feedback Collection:
Background: A city council wanted to gather public opinion on upcoming urban development projects.
Implementation: ChatGPT was embedded into an online public engagement platform. It was trained to provide information on the projects and collect feedback in an organized manner. It could answer questions, provide visual aids, and gauge sentiment in real-time.
Outcome: The council received comprehensive feedback from a larger section of the population than traditional methods. This enriched data aided in more informed decision-making.

4. Educational Support in Public Libraries:

Background: Public libraries were seeking ways to offer academic support to students, especially in research and resource recommendations.
Implementation: Libraries introduced ChatGPT-powered terminals. The model, trained on academic resources, could guide students in research, recommend reading materials, or even clarify academic concepts. It was also made available online, allowing remote access.
Outcome: Students reported improved research quality and efficiency. Libraries experienced increased engagement, both physically and digitally.

5. Emergency Response Coordination:
Background: The national emergency response agency wanted to improve coordination during disasters.
Implementation: A ChatGPT-enhanced communication platform was developed. When emergencies arose, field personnel could communicate with the system to get real-time data, such as safe routes, weather updates, and nearby resources. The system was interconnected with databases from meteorology, traffic control, and other relevant departments.
Outcome: The response time during emergencies improved, with a notable increase in successful operations and coordination efficiency.

Each of these examples emphasizes the adaptability of ChatGPT in diverse government sectors. By understanding specific needs and challenges, governments can customize and integrate AI tools to optimize operations and public service delivery.

CHAPTER 5: CHATGPT FOR CITIZEN INTERACTION

This chapter focuses on using ChatGPT as an interface between the government and citizens, providing services such as citizen inquiries, public service automation, and sentiment analysis on public opinion.

In an age marked by rapid technological advancement and increasing digital interaction, governments across the world are facing the dual challenge of meeting escalating citizen expectations while managing complex public services. AI technologies such as ChatGPT can provide a solution to these challenges, transforming the interaction between the government and its citizens, enhancing service delivery, bolstering the responsiveness of government agencies, and facilitating a more comprehensive understanding of public sentiment.

Handling Citizen Inquiries

Citizen inquiries are one of the most crucial areas of interaction between governments and the people they serve. These inquiries, which span a vast range of topics from policy details to public service information, often require considerable time and resources to address adequately.

ChatGPT can play a transformative role in this context. With its advanced natural language processing capabilities, ChatGPT can serve as an automated response system, accurately answering citizen queries in real-time. This not only increases the speed and efficiency of response but also frees up government personnel to handle more complex issues that require human intervention.

Implementation could involve integrating ChatGPT into government websites or digital platforms as a chatbot or virtual assistant. Unlike traditional customer service models, this AI-driven virtual assistant could provide 24/7 assistance, instantly addressing common inquiries, guiding citizens to relevant resources, or escalating complex issues to human staff. The potential for improving citizen satisfaction through reduced wait times and round-the-clock service is immense.

Automating Public Services

The automation of public services is another area where ChatGPT can make a significant impact. Government agencies often handle repetitive and time-consuming tasks that, while necessary, draw valuable resources away from more strategic initiatives.

ChatGPT, with its ability to understand and generate human-like text, can automate various routine processes. For instance, it can assist citizens in filling out online forms or applications by providing real-time guidance and clarifications. It can generate automated responses to common inquiries, provide information about public programs, or send reminders for upcoming deadlines or appointments.

In automating these processes, ChatGPT can improve the overall efficiency of public services, enhance the citizen experience, and free human staff to focus on tasks that require their unique skills and judgment.

Sentiment Analysis on Public Opinion

Understanding public sentiment is key to the development and implementation of effective public policies and services. Here again, ChatGPT can be a powerful tool. By analyzing data from various sources like social media posts, public forum comments, or survey responses, ChatGPT can provide insights into public sentiment on a range of topics. This kind of analysis can help government agencies gauge public reaction to policies, understand concerns and needs, and gain valuable feedback.

While ChatGPT can provide valuable insights, it is important to adhere to strict ethical guidelines when handling public data. Any personal data should be anonymized, and explicit consent should be obtained where necessary.

In conclusion, ChatGPT's potential to enhance citizen interaction is immense. From handling inquiries to automating services and analyzing sentiment, it promises a transformation in the efficiency and effectiveness of public services. As always, the responsible and ethical use of such AI tools is paramount, ensuring that while we strive for efficiency and innovation, we do not compromise on privacy, fairness, and transparency.

The implementation of ChatGPT for handling citizen inquiries involves several key considerations:

1. **Defining the Scope: While ChatGPT can process a vast amount of data and respond to a wide variety of inquiries, it's essential to clearly define its scope of service. This includes identifying the types of questions it will handle and ensuring it has access to**

up-to-date and accurate information to provide the correct responses.

2. **User Interface Design:** The interface for ChatGPT should be user-friendly and intuitive, designed with the end-user in mind. Citizens should be able to easily access the AI assistant, input their queries, and understand the responses.

3. **Integration with Other Systems:** The AI assistant needs to be integrated seamlessly with other government systems. For instance, if a citizen inquiry requires escalation to a human representative, the system should be able to smoothly transition the conversation, ideally while providing the representative with the context of the inquiry.

4. **Continuous Training and Improvement:** While ChatGPT is pre-trained on a diverse range of data, it should be continuously updated and fine-tuned based on the specific needs and feedback from citizens and the unique context of the government agency. Regular audits should be conducted to assess the accuracy of its responses and to make necessary improvements.

5. **Privacy and Security:** Given that citizens might input personal information while interacting with the AI assistant, robust privacy and security measures should be in place. Personal data should not be stored beyond the active conversation and should not be used to inform future conversations.

In summary, while deploying ChatGPT to handle citizen inquiries can greatly enhance efficiency and citizen satisfaction, its implementation requires careful planning and execution, respecting the principles of Responsible AI. With the right approach, government agencies can harness the power of AI to deliver prompt and accurate responses to citizen inquiries, thereby improving the overall quality of public service.

Implementing ChatGPT for public service automation involves a number of key considerations:

1. **Understanding the Processes: The first step in automation is to thoroughly understand the processes that need to be automated. This includes the steps involved, the rules governing the process, the data required, and the desired outcomes. This understanding forms the foundation for the successful implementation of automation.**

2. **Designing the User Experience: The automation process should be designed to be intuitive and user-friendly. It should reduce the complexity of the process for the user, not add to it. ChatGPT can provide a conversational interface that guides users through the process, asking for necessary information in a natural, conversational manner.**

3. **Integrating with Existing Systems: As with handling citizen inquiries, automating public services requires seamless integration with existing systems. For instance, if a user is filling out a form, the system**

should be able to process that form and provide appropriate responses or actions.

4. **Monitoring and Evaluation:** Regular monitoring and evaluation are crucial to ensure that the automated processes are functioning as intended. Metrics should be established to measure the performance of the automated services, such as the speed of service delivery, the accuracy of the information provided, and user satisfaction.

5. **Privacy and Security:** As automation often involves processing sensitive data, robust privacy and security measures should be implemented. Data should be handled in a secure manner, and users should be informed about how their data will be used and protected.

In conclusion, automating public services using AI like ChatGPT can significantly improve service delivery, save time, and enhance citizen satisfaction. However, it needs to be done in a manner that respects the principles of Responsible AI and places the user at the center of the process. With proper implementation and oversight, public service automation can be a powerful tool for modern, efficient, and citizen-centric government service delivery.

Performing sentiment analysis using AI like ChatGPT involves several steps:

1. **Data Collection:** The first step is to gather the data that will be analyzed. This could include social

media posts, comments on government websites, or responses to public surveys. The data collected should be relevant to the topic of interest and should be as representative as possible of the population whose sentiment is being analyzed.

2. Data Preprocessing: The raw data collected usually needs to be preprocessed before analysis. This could involve removing irrelevant information, dealing with missing data, or transforming the data into a format that the AI can process.

3. Sentiment Analysis: Once the data has been preprocessed, it can be analyzed using ChatGPT. The AI can be trained to identify positive, negative, and neutral sentiments in the text data. More advanced models can also detect more nuanced emotions, such as anger, happiness, or confusion.

4. Interpretation and Action: The results of the sentiment analysis should be interpreted in the context of the original goal. For example, if the analysis was conducted to understand public opinion about a particular policy, the results should be used to inform adjustments to that policy, if needed.

While the potential of sentiment analysis is significant, it's also important to understand its limitations. AI models like ChatGPT are good at detecting patterns in large amounts of data, but they can miss the nuances and subtleties of human language. This is why human oversight is essential when performing sentiment analysis. A human analyst should review the results, consider the context, and ensure that the findings are interpreted correctl

Furthermore, as mentioned before, privacy and ethical considerations must be respected when performing sentiment analysis. Personal data should be anonymized, and data should only be collected and processed with the necessary permissions.

In conclusion, sentiment analysis using AI like ChatGPT can provide valuable insights into public opinion, helping government agencies respond more effectively to the needs and concerns of their citizens. By respecting ethical and privacy considerations and ensuring human oversight, governments can use sentiment analysis responsibly to enhance their understanding of and engagement with the public.

As we conclude this chapter, we must emphasize that the potential of AI tools such as ChatGPT to transform citizen-government interactions is indeed significant. It's not just about enhancing efficiency and productivity within government agencies; it's about reimagining how citizens interact with their government and access public services.

When integrated thoughtfully and ethically, ChatGPT can facilitate streamlined citizen inquiries, offering instant, comprehensive, and personalized responses. By automating repetitive tasks within public service delivery, it can free up valuable human resources for more complex, creative, and citizen-centric tasks. And with its capacity for sentiment analysis, it can empower governments to better understand and respond to the needs and sentiments of their citizens, driving more informed policy-making and more effective communication strategies.

However, as we embrace these possibilities, it is also imperative that we maintain a strong commitment to ethical AI practices.

Privacy must always be respected. In practice, this means implementing strict data handling procedures and ensuring any personal data used or generated in the course of using ChatGPT is adequately protected. When AI is used to interact directly with citizens, informed consent and transparency become even more crucial.

Fairness is another key consideration. This involves constant vigilance for any signs of bias in how ChatGPT handles citizen inquiries or automates services, and a commitment to rectifying such bias where it appears.

Transparency should underpin all AI use in government-citizen interactions. Citizens should be aware when they are interacting with an AI, understand how decisions are being made, and have clear channels to challenge decisions or seek further information.

In the next chapter, we will continue to explore the potential applications of ChatGPT in government, turning our attention to its role in policymaking. As always, our focus will be on harnessing the power of AI for public good while maintaining a strong commitment to ethical and responsible AI use.

EXAMPLES:

1. Biases in Decision-making:
***Scenario*: A local government decided to use ChatGPT as a tool to screen applications for small business grants. The idea was to expedite the application review process.**
***Issue*: It was soon discovered that businesses owned by certain minority groups were receiving fewer grant approvals. Upon investigation, it was found that the historical data used to train ChatGPT had unintentional biases due to systemic discrimination in past grant allocations.**
***Implications*: Relying blindly on AI without checking for inherent biases can perpetuate and even amplify systemic discrimination. It's crucial to continually evaluate and refine models to ensure fairness.**

2. Privacy Concerns in Public Health:
***Scenario*: A healthcare department implemented ChatGPT to answer queries about personal health issues.**
***Issue*: Even though the system was designed to forget the questions after answering, concerns arose about the potential misuse of sensitive health data. Some users were unaware that their queries were being processed by an AI, expecting human-level confidentiality.**
***Implications*: Privacy considerations, especially concerning health and personal data, are paramount. Clear communication about how data is processed and stored is vital for public trust.**

3. Dependence and Job Displacement:
***Scenario*: A government tax department incorporated ChatGPT to handle taxpayer inquiries, reducing the need for human customer service representatives.**

Issue: While efficiency improved, there was significant job displacement. Additionally, as people grew dependent on ChatGPT for immediate answers, the depth and nuance that human agents provided began to be overlooked.
Implications: While AI can enhance efficiency, it's vital to consider the human element. Balancing automation with human intuition and judgment is crucial.

4. Misinformation in Public Communication:
Scenario: A city council utilized ChatGPT for disseminating information about local policies and events.
Issue: Occasionally, ChatGPT would provide outdated or slightly inaccurate information due to the vast amount of data it was trained on, leading to public confusion or misinformation.
Implications: Accuracy is crucial in public communication. While AI can process vast amounts of data, there needs to be a system in place to ensure the currency and accuracy of the information disseminated.

5. Over-reliance on AI in Critical Decision-making:
Scenario: A traffic management department integrated ChatGPT to assist in real-time traffic control decisions based on various data inputs.
Issue: During a major event, the system suggested a traffic routing that, while efficient on paper, failed to consider a recent, unplanned road closure, causing significant traffic congestion.
Implications: While AI can analyze data at unparalleled speeds, there's a risk in over-relying on it for critical decisions. Real-time human oversight and judgment are often necessary to consider unanticipated factors.

These examples emphasize that while ChatGPT and similar AI tools have immense potential in government applications, there are inherent risks. Ethical considerations should be at the forefront of any AI integration to ensure that technology serves the public good responsibly.

CHAPTER 6: CHATGPT IN POLICY MAKING

Here, we discuss how ChatGPT can be used to assist in policy-making processes, including information gathering, policy drafting, and simulating policy outcomes based on large sets of data.

Policy making is one of the most crucial functions of government. It requires a delicate balance of data analysis, stakeholder input, strategic planning, and legislative crafting. In this complex and critical process, AI technologies like ChatGPT can be utilized as powerful tools to increase efficiency, enhance precision, and promote inclusivity.

1. **Information Gathering**

The inception of any policy-making process lies in information gathering. Policymakers need to delve into a plethora of sources, including research papers, existing legislation, and public opinion, to gather relevant data and insights. This process, while essential, can be laborious and time-consuming.

ChatGPT, with its advanced language processing capabilities, can expedite this process by sifting through vast amounts of textual data, identifying key trends and summarizing salient points. For instance, it can scan and synthesize information from a multitude of research papers on a specific subject, present overviews of existing legislation, or analyze social media posts to gauge public sentiment.

While leveraging AI for information gathering, it is crucial to be mindful of data bias. The data fed into ChatGPT should be as representative and unbiased as possible to ensure the information it provides accurately reflects the reality.

2. Policy Drafting

After gathering the necessary information, the next step in the policy-making process is the drafting of policy documents. Here, ChatGPT can be of significant assistance. Given an outline or specific instructions, ChatGPT can generate initial drafts of policy documents, saving policy makers considerable time and effort. Additionally, it can also help maintain the consistency and clarity of policy language, thus enhancing the overall quality of the document.

Despite its capabilities, the drafts produced by ChatGPT should serve as a starting point. Human expertise is still crucial to review, refine, and approve these drafts to ensure they accurately reflect the policy objectives and cater to the complexities and nuances of real-world policy-making.

3. Simulating Policy Outcomes

One of the unique applications of AI in policy-making is its ability to simulate potential policy outcomes. ChatGPT, when combined with other machine learning models and provided with large datasets, can help predict the possible impacts of policy decisions.

For instance, based on historical and current data, these models can project how a new educational policy might affect literacy rates or how changes in healthcare legislation might impact public health outcomes. These simulations can provide policymakers with valuable

insights, allowing them to tweak policies before implementation to ensure the best possible results.

However, it's important to interpret these simulations cautiously. They are based on the data they're fed and the assumptions they're built on, and hence, they should be viewed as approximations and not absolute predictions.

In conclusion, AI technologies like ChatGPT hold significant potential in enhancing the policy-making process. They offer opportunities for increased efficiency, enhanced accuracy, and broader inclusivity. However, it's essential to balance these benefits against potential pitfalls, such as data bias or over-reliance on AI, and to uphold the principles of Responsible AI in every stage of policy-making. As we continue to leverage AI in government functions, these principles should be at the forefront of our considerations.

Information gathering is a critical first step in the policy-making process, enabling decision-makers to understand the landscape of the issue at hand. It involves collecting and processing a myriad of data types from a multitude of sources. AI systems like ChatGPT, with their advanced text processing capabilities, can significantly enhance this information gathering process.

1. Processing Academic Research: ChatGPT can be utilized to read, comprehend, and synthesize vast amounts of academic literature. Given its ability to understand natural language, it can delve into articles, research papers, studies, and reports, summarizing key points and extracting relevant

insights. This can help policymakers get a handle on the current academic consensus on the issue at hand, without having to read through the entirety of the literature themselves.

2. Analyzing Existing Legislation: In addition to academic research, it's also important to understand the existing legislative landscape. ChatGPT can assist by processing large volumes of legal and policy documents, extracting their key provisions, and comparing them to help policy makers understand what has already been implemented and how effective it has been.

3. Gauging Public Opinion: Public sentiment plays a crucial role in shaping policies. ChatGPT can assist in gauging public opinion by analyzing data from various sources, such as social media posts, comments on public forums, and responses to surveys. By doing so, it can identify patterns, trends, and sentiments related to the policy issue, providing valuable insights to policymakers.

4. Identifying Stakeholder Positions: Policies often involve a variety of stakeholders with differing perspectives. ChatGPT can assist in identifying these perspectives by processing statements, articles, and other documents published by these stakeholders. This can help in understanding the different arguments and positions related to the policy issue.

However, while leveraging AI for information gathering, it's important to ensure that the data used is comprehensive, representative, and unbiased. The information provided by ChatGPT is only as good as the data it's trained on. Therefore, any biases in the data, whether in terms of what's included or excluded, can skew the insights generated.

Furthermore, while AI can dramatically speed up the information gathering process and provide valuable insights, it is not a replacement for human judgement. Policymakers should critically evaluate the insights provided by AI, using them as one of many tools in their decision-making toolkit.

In conclusion, AI can play a transformative role in the information gathering stage of policy-making, reducing the time and effort required and providing diverse and valuable insights. However, this process must be carefully managed to ensure data quality and representativeness, and the insights generated must be critically evaluated by human decision-makers.

Policy drafting is a crucial part of the policy-making process. This is where the insights gathered from various sources and stakeholders are transformed into a cohesive, actionable document. The use of AI technologies like ChatGPT can greatly assist in this process.

1. Draft Generation: ChatGPT, with its natural language processing capabilities, can generate initial drafts of policy documents based on provided guidelines, existing legislation, academic research, and stakeholder positions. For example, if tasked with drafting a policy document on climate change,

ChatGPT could take into account the relevant international agreements, existing national legislation, latest academic research, and public opinion data to generate a comprehensive first draft. This can drastically reduce the time and effort required for this task.

2. Language Consistency and Clarity: Drafting policy documents requires not only content accuracy but also clear and consistent language. Policies must be understandable to a wide audience and free from any ambiguity. ChatGPT can help ensure this by reviewing and revising drafts to achieve clear and consistent language. It can help avoid jargon, ensure active voice, and maintain a consistent tone and style throughout the document.

3. Reference and Fact Checking: As part of the drafting process, ChatGPT can also assist in fact-checking and ensuring proper referencing. Given its ability to process vast amounts of information quickly, it can verify statements against the source data and ensure that all claims are properly supported and referenced.

However, while ChatGPT can significantly speed up the policy drafting process and enhance the quality of the output, it is essential that the AI-generated drafts are reviewed by human policy makers. They need to ensure the draft aligns with the policy objectives, respects the relevant legal and ethical constraints, and considers the nuances and complexities of the real-world environment.

AI is an assistive tool in this process, not a replacement for human judgement.

In conclusion, AI can significantly enhance the policy drafting process, making it more efficient and potentially improving the quality of the drafts. However, the use of AI in policy drafting should be carefully managed, and the outputs should always be subject to human review and judgement.

Simulating policy outcomes is a complex but crucial aspect of the policy-making process. Policymakers need to anticipate the potential impacts of their decisions to the best of their ability. AI, and specifically models like ChatGPT, can greatly aid this process when appropriately applied.

1. Scenario Simulation: ChatGPT, when combined with other AI models such as deep learning algorithms or predictive analytics tools, can simulate a variety of policy scenarios based on available data. For instance, a policy to increase taxes on carbon emissions could have various outcomes - from reducing greenhouse gas emissions to potentially impacting certain industries adversely. AI can help simulate these outcomes, providing policymakers with a range of possible scenarios that might result from their decisions.

2. Outcome Forecasting: Apart from simulating scenarios, AI models can also forecast potential policy outcomes. For example, using historical and current data on population health and healthcare

provision, AI can help predict the potential impact of changes in healthcare policies on public health outcomes. Such forecasting can offer valuable insights to policymakers, enabling them to fine-tune their policies for optimal results.

3. **Decision Support:** These simulations and forecasts can form an essential part of the decision support systems for policymakers. By providing data-driven insights and predictions, AI can help policymakers weigh the pros and cons of different policy options and make more informed decisions.

However, while AI can enhance the policy-making process by providing data-driven simulations and forecasts, it's crucial to handle these tools with caution. They are based on algorithms that are as good as the data they are fed and the assumptions they're built upon. AI simulations should not be seen as crystal balls providing definitive predictions, but rather as tools providing informed approximations that can guide decision-making.

It's also important to remember that while AI can provide quantitative forecasts, the qualitative aspects of policy impact - such as social equity or ethical implications - also need to be considered, and these are areas where human judgement is indispensable.

In conclusion, AI can be a powerful tool in simulating policy outcomes and supporting policy decisions, but it should be used judiciously and complemented with human expertise and judgement.

In conclusion, AI technologies like ChatGPT are opening up new avenues for improving the policy-making process. These technologies, when appropriately implemented, can assist in handling the enormous amounts of information needed for informed policy decisions, streamlining the drafting process, and simulating the potential impacts of policy decisions, thus allowing for a more efficient, accurate, and inclusive policy-making process.

However, with these significant advantages come important considerations. Key among these is the risk of data bias. AI systems, including ChatGPT, are trained on large datasets and their outputs are based on the patterns and trends they learn from this data. If the training data is biased, the AI's outputs could also be biased, potentially leading to skewed or unfair policy decisions. It is therefore crucial to ensure the use of fair and representative data in the AI training process.

Another concern is the potential for over-reliance on AI in policy making. While AI can help streamline processes and provide valuable insights, human judgement and expertise remain essential. Policy decisions often involve complex social, economic, and ethical considerations that AI systems are currently unable to fully comprehend. Policymakers should therefore use AI as a tool to inform and support their decisions, rather than as a replacement for human judgement.

Finally, the principles of Responsible AI - transparency, fairness, privacy, and security - should guide the use of AI in policy making. Policymakers should be transparent about how they're using AI and what data the AI is

processing. They should ensure that the AI's use is fair and does not lead to discrimination or bias. They should also uphold privacy by anonymizing data and using robust security measures to protect data from breaches.

In the next chapter, we will delve into the role of AI in public sector decision-making, exploring how AI technologies like ChatGPT can be used to support decisions in various areas of public administration. This will provide further insights into the potential of AI to transform government operations, as well as the considerations that need to guide its responsible use.

EXAMPLES:

1. Multi-lingual Support for Diverse Communities:
***Scenario*: In a multicultural city with residents speaking multiple languages, the local government wanted to deploy ChatGPT for their citizen query system.**
***Deployment Strategy*: They implemented a version of ChatGPT trained in multiple languages to cater to the city's diverse linguistic landscape.**
***Outcome*: Residents, regardless of their primary language, could effectively communicate with the system and get accurate, timely responses to their queries. The government saw a spike in positive user feedback and a significant reduction in language-related complaints.**
***Best Practice*: Tailor AI deployments to cater to the unique demographic and linguistic characteristics of the community it serves.**

2. ChatGPT in Emergency Response:

Scenario: A coastal town frequently affected by natural calamities wanted to improve its emergency response mechanism.
Deployment Strategy: The local administration integrated ChatGPT into their emergency response helpline, training it on disaster-related queries and providing real-time data about shelter locations, medical aid centers, and evacuation routes.
Outcome: During a subsequent hurricane, residents received immediate and accurate guidance, resulting in more effective evacuations and fewer casualties.
Best Practice: When deploying AI in critical sectors, ensure the system is trained on highly relevant, localized data and is integrated seamlessly into the existing infrastructure.

3. Integrating Feedback Mechanisms:
Scenario: A national tax agency introduced ChatGPT to answer queries related to tax filing but was concerned about potential misinformation.
Deployment Strategy: Along with ChatGPT, a feedback mechanism was embedded, allowing users to rate answers and provide comments. This feedback was reviewed weekly.
Outcome: Over time, the system's accuracy improved significantly based on user feedback, and the agency could address frequently reported issues proactively.
Best Practice: Continuous improvement is vital. Embedding feedback mechanisms ensures the system evolves based on real-world user interactions.

4. Phased Deployment in Healthcare:
Scenario: A public health department was eager to use ChatGPT for patient queries but wary of potential risks.

Deployment Strategy: They adopted a phased approach. Initially, ChatGPT was deployed in non-critical areas, like appointment scheduling and general health queries. Once it proved reliable, its role expanded to more sensitive areas, always under human oversight.
Outcome: Mistakes and teething issues were caught early and rectified without significant repercussions. The system eventually became a vital tool for the department, handling a broad spectrum of queries.
Best Practice: Especially in sensitive sectors, a phased deployment approach minimizes risks and allows for iterative improvements.

5. Cross-departmental Integration:
Scenario: A city wanted to create a one-stop digital portal for all citizen services, from utilities and permits to event information.
Deployment Strategy: Different departments collaborated to integrate their databases and services into a unified system, with ChatGPT serving as the primary interface, answering queries and directing users to the right department or service.
Outcome: Citizens no longer had to navigate multiple websites or face bureaucratic hurdles. They had a single, intuitive interface that catered to most of their needs.
Best Practice: Encourage inter-departmental collaboration when deploying AI solutions to provide more holistic and user-friendly services.

These examples underline the importance of thoughtful deployment strategies tailored to the specific needs and challenges of government sectors.

CHAPTER 7: MONITORING AND EVALUATION OF CHATGPT USE

This chapter guides on ways to assess the effectiveness and efficiency of ChatGPT in government use. Topics covered include setting key performance indicators, regular auditing, feedback collection, and continual improvement of AI systems.

Setting Key Performance Indicators

Key Performance Indicators (KPIs) serve as a practical tool for measuring the effectiveness and efficiency of a system. KPIs for AI systems like ChatGPT can be divided into several categories, including system performance, user satisfaction, and overall organizational impact.

1. System Performance: These KPIs focus on the technical functioning of ChatGPT, such as accuracy in understanding and responding to queries, speed of response, and system availability and reliability.

2. User Satisfaction: User feedback is crucial in assessing the practical utility and usability of ChatGPT. This could be measured through surveys or direct feedback mechanisms, focusing on elements like the relevance of the responses, ease of use, and user's overall satisfaction.

3. Organizational Impact: These KPIs assess the broader impact of ChatGPT on the organization, including cost savings, increased operational efficiency, and improvement in service delivery.

Conducting Regular Audits

Regular auditing of ChatGPT's performance is essential to maintain system integrity, fairness, and transparency. Audits should check for any biases in data or AI's decision-making process, adherence to privacy standards, and system security. These audits should be performed by a combination of internal and external auditors to ensure impartiality and thoroughness.

Feedback Collection

Feedback is a vital component of any monitoring and evaluation process. Governments should establish a regular feedback collection mechanism for both internal (staff) and external (public) users. Feedback can be obtained through multiple channels - online surveys, public consultations, focus group discussions, etc. This feedback should be carefully analyzed and incorporated into subsequent system improvements.

Continual Improvement of AI Systems

AI systems are continually evolving and learning. Therefore, governments need to foster a culture of continuous improvement, based on lessons learned from performance data, audit findings, and user feedback. This includes regular updates to the system to improve its functionalities, addressing biases, improving data security, and refining the system based on advancements in AI technology and ethics.

In Conclusion

Monitoring and evaluation are not mere afterthoughts, but integral parts of using AI systems like ChatGPT. It ensures that the system delivers its intended benefits, stays aligned with the ethical principles of fairness, transparency, and privacy, and continuously improves over time. As the use of AI expands in government, maintaining a robust monitoring and evaluation system will become increasingly important to build public trust and to achieve the goal of responsible AI use.

If the goal is to improve citizen satisfaction, a KPI could be the satisfaction rate as measured by surveys or feedback forms. If cost reduction or efficiency improvement is the objective, KPIs could be the reduction in the cost per inquiry handled, or the number of inquiries resolved without human intervention.
In addition to these outcome-oriented KPIs, it's also useful to track process-oriented KPIs that measure the functioning and usage of ChatGPT. For example:

1. Usage Statistics: This includes metrics like the number of queries handled by ChatGPT, the number of unique users, or the frequency of use. These metrics can provide insights into the acceptance and adoption of ChatGPT by users.

2. Accuracy Metrics: This measures how accurately ChatGPT understands and responds to queries. This can be tracked by analyzing a random sample of interactions and determining the percentage in which ChatGPT provided an accurate and useful response.

3. System Performance: This includes metrics like system uptime, speed of response, and error rates. These metrics help to assess the technical performance of the system.

Setting KPIs provides a tangible way to track the performance of ChatGPT over time and measure its impact. However, it's important to regularly review and update these KPIs to ensure they continue to align with the evolving objectives and priorities of the government agency.

By consistently monitoring and evaluating these KPIs, government agencies can ensure that they are making effective use of ChatGPT, and continually improving its implementation to better serve their objectives.

For auditing ChatGPT's use in a government context, three main areas should be considered:

1. Data Audit: This involves reviewing the data used to train and operate ChatGPT. The goal is to identify any potential biases or inaccuracies in the data, which could lead to biased or inaccurate outputs. For instance, if ChatGPT is trained primarily on data from a specific demographic group, it may not perform as well when interacting with individuals outside of that group.

2. Process Audit: This involves examining the processes used to implement and operate ChatGPT. For example, is the system being used in the intended manner? Are there procedures in place for handling exceptions or errors? Are user privacy and data security measures effectively implemented and followed? Process audits can identify operational issues that may affect the performance or trustworthiness of the AI system.

3. Output Audit: This involves reviewing the outputs generated by ChatGPT. For instance, are the responses accurate and appropriate? Are there any patterns of bias or error in the outputs? Output audits can highlight issues with the AI system's performance, helping to pinpoint areas for improvement.

It's also important to involve multiple stakeholders in the audit process, including technical experts, end users, and possibly independent third parties. This ensures a comprehensive and balanced evaluation of the AI system.

In conclusion, regular auditing is an essential part of monitoring and evaluating AI use in government. It helps to ensure that AI systems like ChatGPT are performing as intended, and that they are upholding important principles like fairness, transparency, and privacy. By identifying and addressing issues promptly, regular audits can help maintain public trust in the use of AI in government.

Collecting feedback is a critical aspect of the monitoring and evaluation process of implementing AI systems like ChatGPT within governmental organizations. It helps the organization understand the user's perspective on the effectiveness and user-friendliness of the AI system. Here's a more in-depth look at how feedback collection can be effectively performed:

Internal Feedback:

Government staff members who directly interact with ChatGPT form an important group for feedback collection. Their firsthand experience with the system can provide valuable insights about the AI's efficiency, accuracy, and usability. This feedback can be collected through various methods, such as one-on-one interviews, focus group discussions, or anonymous online surveys.

Internal feedback should be aimed at understanding the user experience, such as:

- How helpful is ChatGPT in aiding employees with their tasks?
- How intuitive is the user interface?
- Are there any challenges or issues encountered while using ChatGPT?
- Are there specific areas where they believe improvements can be made?

External Feedback:

External feedback comes from citizens who interact with the AI system, often through public-facing platforms. This feedback helps gauge citizen satisfaction and the AI's effectiveness in addressing their needs.

Ways to collect external feedback can include online surveys, feedback forms on the government website, social media sentiment analysis, or public consultations. This feedback can provide insights into:

- The overall satisfaction of citizens with their interaction with ChatGPT.
- The clarity and accuracy of the AI's responses.

- The usefulness of the AI in helping citizens find information or complete tasks.
- Areas where citizens feel the system could be improved or expanded.

In conclusion, both internal and external feedback are key to understanding how ChatGPT is perceived and how well it's serving its intended purpose. Regular collection and analysis of this feedback provide an ongoing source of insights that can be used to continually refine and improve the system, thereby ensuring it remains effective and beneficial for its users.

AI systems like ChatGPT are dynamic by nature and have an inherent potential for continual learning and improvement. This process is not automatic; it requires ongoing assessment, feedback interpretation, and the incorporation of new developments in AI technology and ethical guidelines. Here is a deeper exploration of the process of continual improvement in AI systems:

Performance Data Driven Improvements:

Key Performance Indicators (KPIs) and other performance metrics provide crucial quantitative data on how the AI system is functioning. They can reveal areas where the system is excelling and where it is falling short. For example, if the response time of ChatGPT to citizen queries is identified as a KPI, and data shows that this is consistently longer than desired, then this indicates a need for improvement in the system's responsiveness.

Incorporating Audit Findings:

Regular audits of the AI system provide valuable insights into its functioning and adherence to fairness, privacy, and security standards. Findings from these audits should be used to make necessary modifications to the AI system. For example, if an audit reveals a bias in the AI's responses towards a particular demographic, steps should be taken to rectify this bias and ensure fairness.

Using User Feedback:

As discussed earlier, feedback from users, both internal and external, is a rich source of qualitative data on the user experience with the AI system. This feedback can highlight strengths and weaknesses in the system from the user's perspective, and can guide improvements to make the system more user-friendly and effective.

Adapting to AI Advancements and Ethical Considerations:

The field of AI is rapidly evolving, with new technologies and techniques being developed continuously. Government agencies should stay abreast of these developments and assess how they can be harnessed to improve their AI systems.

Similarly, the understanding of ethical considerations in AI use is also evolving. Issues like bias, privacy, transparency, and accountability are the subject of ongoing research and discussion. As ethical standards and guidelines evolve, these should be incorporated into the AI system's design and use.

In conclusion, the process of continual improvement of AI systems is crucial for ensuring that these systems remain effective, fair, and relevant over time. It requires a commitment to ongoing monitoring and evaluation, a willingness to learn from data and feedback, and a readiness to adapt to new developments in the field of AI.

The deployment of artificial intelligence (AI) systems like ChatGPT within government operations necessitates rigorous monitoring and evaluation. The aim of this is twofold: to maximize the benefits and to mitigate the risks associated with AI technology. Responsible AI, which is an approach to AI use that prioritizes ethics, fairness, transparency, and accountability, demands continuous attention to these aspects. To that end, setting clear KPIs, regular auditing, proactive feedback collection, and fostering a culture of continual improvement are crucial.

Setting Clear KPIs:

Key performance indicators provide an objective measure of the AI system's effectiveness. They enable governments to quantify and track progress toward specific goals. When KPIs are clearly defined and directly linked to the objectives of using AI, they can effectively guide development and identify areas where improvement is needed.

Regular analysis of KPIs can ensure the AI system is delivering on its intended purpose, be it improving service delivery speed, enhancing citizen satisfaction, or increasing staff productivity.

Conducting Regular Audits:

Regular audits ensure the AI system is not just efficient but also fair and accountable. These audits go beyond measuring performance against KPIs and delve into the system's operational details. They scrutinize the data used, the decisions made, and the processes followed by the AI, ensuring that biases, privacy breaches, or security vulnerabilities are detected and addressed promptly.

Collecting and Acting on User Feedback:

Feedback from both internal and external users is a treasure trove of insights. It sheds light on the user experience, the system's usability, and areas needing improvement. By proactively collecting feedback through surveys, user interviews, or public consultations, governments can gauge the effectiveness of the AI system from a user perspective. It's equally important to act on this feedback, translating it into tangible improvements in the system.

Fostering a Culture of Continual Improvement:

AI systems should not be viewed as static entities but rather as dynamic tools with potential for continuous learning and improvement. The drive for continual improvement should be guided by insights drawn from performance data, audit findings, and user feedback. Moreover, it should involve staying current with the latest advancements in AI technology and ethics, assimilating new opportunities for enhancement, and addressing emerging ethical considerations.

In conclusion, as AI technologies continue to evolve and their use in government expands, the role of effective monitoring and evaluation becomes increasingly vital. The practices outlined above—setting clear KPIs, conducting regular audits, collecting and acting on user feedback, and fostering a culture of continual improvement—are key to achieving responsible, effective, and ethical use of AI in public service. By rigorously following these practices, governments can ensure they are harnessing the full benefits of AI like ChatGPT, while responsibly managing its risks and maintaining public trust.

EXAMPLES"

1. Customer Service Enhancement in Public Transport:
Scenario: A metropolitan city's public transportation authority was receiving an overwhelming number of inquiries daily, leading to long wait times and frustrated commuters.
Implementation: ChatGPT was integrated into the transport authority's website and mobile app to instantly answer queries related to schedules, fare costs, and route disruptions.
Impact: The time taken to address a query reduced by 80%. Additionally, the cost associated with customer service staffing reduced by 30%, with the staff now focusing on more complex issues beyond ChatGPT's scope.
ROI: The investment in ChatGPT was recouped within a year due to staff cost reductions and improved commuter satisfaction leading to increased use of public transportation.

2. Simplifying Tax Filing:

Scenario: The national tax department noticed that many citizens were making errors in their tax filings or reaching out frequently with similar questions.
Implementation: ChatGPT was implemented on the tax department's online portal, trained to guide users through the filing process step-by-step and answer common questions.
Impact: Errors in tax filings decreased by 40%, and calls to the tax department's helpline reduced by 60%.
ROI: The reduced need for manual review of filings and the decrease in helpline operating costs led to substantial savings, with the ChatGPT system paying for itself within eight months.

3. Health Awareness Campaigns:
Scenario: A regional health department aimed to raise awareness about seasonal diseases and vaccination schedules but faced challenges in effectively disseminating information.
Implementation: ChatGPT was deployed on the health department's website and social media, offering instant answers to public queries about diseases, symptoms, precautions, and nearby vaccination centers.
Impact: There was a 50% increase in the number of people getting vaccinated on time, and a significant reduction in seasonal disease outbreaks.
ROI: The cost savings from fewer disease outbreaks and related hospitalizations far outweighed the investment in the ChatGPT system.

4. Efficient Licensing and Permit Issuance:

Scenario: A city's administrative office was swamped with inquiries about permits and licenses, from business operations to home renovations.
Implementation: ChatGPT was introduced on the city's administrative portal to guide users through the permit application process, clarify requirements, and provide status updates.
Impact: Application errors dropped by 70%, expediting the approval process, and face-to-face appointments decreased by 50%, freeing up staff time.
ROI: Operational efficiency led to faster permit approvals, promoting local businesses and home renovations. The positive economic impact, combined with reduced administrative costs, ensured the initiative was ROI-positive within a year.

5. Environmental Conservation Education:E
Scenario: An environmental agency wanted to educate the public about conservation efforts, recycling practices, and report environmental violations.
Implementation: ChatGPT was set up on the agency's website and in community centers, equipped to provide information on best environmental practices and accept violation reports.
Impact: Recycling rates in the city increased by 30%, and there was a noticeable improvement in public participation in conservation programs.
ROI: The long-term benefits of a more environmentally-conscious community, reduced waste management costs, and improved public spaces ensured a substantial return on the agency's ChatGPT investment.

These examples showcase the tangible benefits and the financial ROI of implementing ChatGPT in various government sectors. The combination of improved efficiency, reduced costs, and better public outcomes emphasizes the transformative potential of such AI integrations.

CHAPTER 8: TRAINING AND CAPACITY BUILDING

Training government personnel to use ChatGPT effectively is essential. This chapter covers developing training programs, addressing skill gaps, and promoting an AI-positive culture within the government.

Developing Training Programs

The adoption of AI technologies like ChatGPT in government operations necessitates tailored training programs to equip the personnel with the knowledge and skills required to effectively use these tools. Such programs should be designed based on the needs of different roles within the organization.

Frontline workers who directly interact with the AI systems might require in-depth operational training, while policy makers and decision-makers might benefit from a broader, strategic understanding of how AI can enhance their work. For IT staff, training might focus more on system integration, data management, and troubleshooting.

Training programs should not only cover the technical aspects but also delve into ethical considerations, privacy protection, and responsible AI use. They should be dynamic and updated regularly to incorporate the latest developments in AI technology and ethical guidelines. Importantly, these programs should also be designed to foster confidence and comfort in using AI systems, helping to address any concerns or apprehensions staff may have.

Addressing Skill Gaps

The integration of AI in public sector work often requires a new set of skills. It's essential to identify these skill gaps within the workforce and take proactive measures to bridge them. This can be achieved through various methods including hiring new personnel with expertise in AI, offering upskilling opportunities or training programs for existing staff, and forming collaborations with academia or industry for knowledge sharing and training.

Moreover, it's important to recognize the multidisciplinary nature of AI application. Creating interdisciplinary teams comprising of domain experts, data scientists, ethicists, and IT specialists can result in more effective and responsible AI use.

Promoting an AI-positive Culture

A successful AI transformation within government organizations is not just about introducing new technologies, but also about fostering an AI-positive culture. This involves encouraging curiosity and learning about AI, promoting its responsible use, and emphasizing its role as a tool to aid, not replace, human personnel.

Leadership plays a crucial role in shaping this culture. By openly advocating for AI's benefits, addressing concerns transparently, and encouraging ongoing learning and ethical AI use, leaders can help build trust and confidence in these technologies.

Conclusion

Training and capacity building are critical when introducing AI technologies like ChatGPT in government operations. Through tailored training programs, proactive efforts to address skill gaps, and a focus on creating an AI-positive culture, government organizations can better equip their personnel to leverage AI responsibly and effectively. As AI technologies continue to advance, ongoing learning and capacity building will remain key to adapting and maximizing the potential of these tools.

Addressing Skill Gaps

Addressing skill gaps is crucial when adopting new AI technologies like ChatGPT in government operations. Staff at all levels should have the necessary knowledge and skills to use these tools effectively.

1. Skills Assessment: The first step in addressing skill gaps is to conduct a comprehensive skills assessment to identify areas where training is needed. This assessment should cover technical skills related to the use of the AI system, as well as softer skills like understanding AI ethics and interpreting AI outputs.

2. Upskilling and Reskilling: Once the skill gaps are identified, upskilling and reskilling programs should be initiated. Upskilling refers to training staff to acquire new skills related to their current roles, while reskilling involves training staff for new roles that have emerged due to the adoption of AI.

3. Recruitment and Collaboration: In some cases, it might be necessary to recruit new personnel with AI expertise. Alternatively, governments could consider forming collaborations with academia or industry to access expert knowledge and skills.

Promoting an AI-Positive Culture

The successful integration of AI tools like ChatGPT into government operations relies not only on technical and skills training but also on fostering an AI-positive culture. This involves creating an environment where curiosity, innovation, and responsible use of AI are encouraged.

1. Leadership Commitment: Leadership commitment is crucial in promoting an AI-positive culture. Leaders should be vocal advocates of AI's benefits and should lead by example in the ethical and responsible use of AI.

2. Transparency and Communication: Clear, open, and transparent communication about the purpose, use, and benefits of AI can help build trust and acceptance among staff.

3. Encourage Innovation and Learning: Government organizations should encourage a culture of innovation and continual learning. Regular training sessions, workshops, or seminars on AI can help keep staff up-to-date with the latest advancements and best practices.

In conclusion, a comprehensive approach to training and capacity building can ensure the effective use of AI tools like ChatGPT in government operations. By focusing on developing tailored training programs, addressing skill gaps, and fostering an AI-positive culture, governments can ensure that their staff are well-prepared to harness the benefits of AI.

Promoting an AI-Positive Culture

Promoting an AI-positive culture within the government is a fundamental aspect of successful AI implementation. An AI-positive culture can help alleviate any fear or apprehension about AI technologies, encourage the adoption of new tools like ChatGPT, and stimulate innovative thinking.

1. **Leadership Role: Leadership plays a crucial role in shaping the organization's culture. Leaders should demonstrate an understanding and acceptance of AI technologies, articulate a clear vision for how AI can benefit their agency, and commit to ethical and responsible AI use.**

2. **Education and Awareness: Regular training sessions, workshops, and seminars can help increase understanding of AI technologies, demystify common misconceptions, and foster a sense of enthusiasm and curiosity. Government agencies should also ensure that their staff are aware of the ethical considerations related to AI use and understand their responsibilities in this regard.**

3. **Encouraging Innovation: Creating a culture that encourages experimentation and accepts failure as part of the learning process can stimulate innovative uses of AI. Government agencies should provide opportunities for staff to propose and test new AI applications, and should recognize and celebrate successful innovations.**

4. **Open Communication:** An open dialogue about the benefits, challenges, and ethical implications of AI can foster trust and acceptance among staff. Governments should encourage questions and discussions about AI, and should be transparent about how AI systems like ChatGPT are being used, what decisions are being automated, and what measures are in place to ensure fairness and accountability.

In conclusion, promoting an AI-positive culture is as crucial as technical training in ensuring the effective and responsible use of AI technologies like ChatGPT in government. By committing to education, openness, and innovation, governments can foster a culture that embraces the opportunities of AI while being mindful of its challenges.

Incentivizing Learning and Experimentation:

To create a truly AI-positive culture, it's crucial to incentivize learning and experimentation with AI tools like ChatGPT. Employees should feel encouraged to engage with these technologies, test new applications, and seek out ways to optimize their use. This could be facilitated through formal reward structures, opportunities for skill-building, or the creation of innovation labs where employees can experiment with AI tools.

Addressing Concerns and Fears:

Addressing concerns and fears about AI is another key aspect of fostering an AI-positive culture. It's essential to have open and honest discussions about job security, privacy, and other issues that employees might be concerned about. Assurances should be given that AI is there to augment human capabilities, not replace them, and that robust measures are in place to protect privacy and ensure responsible AI use.

Emphasizing Ethics and Responsibility:

Finally, promoting an AI-positive culture also involves emphasizing ethics and responsibility in AI use. This means not just training employees on how to use AI tools, but also educating them about the ethical considerations and their responsibilities when using these tools. Regular discussions, trainings, or workshops on AI ethics can help embed these considerations into everyday work practices.

In conclusion, promoting an AI-positive culture in government requires leadership support, incentives for learning and experimentation, open discussions about concerns, and an emphasis on ethics and responsibility. By fostering such a culture, governments can ensure that AI technologies like ChatGPT are used effectively and responsibly, maximizing their benefits for public service.

Indeed, as AI continues to proliferate in various sectors of society, it's paramount for government agencies to stay ahead of the curve. Training and capacity building are crucial not just to get the maximum benefit out of AI applications but also to address the ethical and societal implications that accompany these technologies.

The effective use of AI in government services hinges on a deep understanding of how AI works, how to use it effectively, and how to navigate the risks and rewards that come with it. This requires comprehensive and ongoing training programs that adapt to technological advancements and changing societal contexts. These programs should not only equip employees with the necessary technical skills but also foster critical thinking and ethical reasoning.

Addressing skill gaps is another pivotal aspect of AI integration in government services. As AI technologies become more sophisticated, they demand a wider range of skills – from data analysis to policy formulation. Therefore, governments need to take a proactive approach in identifying these skill gaps and developing strategies to bridge them, whether through upskilling programs, collaborations with academia or industry, or hiring new talent.

Finally, creating an AI-positive culture within the government can go a long way in maximizing the benefits of AI technologies like ChatGPT. By creating an environment that encourages learning, innovation, and ethical use of AI, governments can ensure that their personnel are not only comfortable using AI tools, but are also motivated to find new ways to leverage them for public service.

In the era of digital transformation, AI technologies present significant opportunities for governments to improve their services, make informed decisions, and better connect with their citizens. By investing in training

and capacity building, governments can position themselves to harness these opportunities, driving forward a future where AI is a key enabler of efficient, effective, and equitable public service.

EXAMPLES:

1. Virtual Training Modules for Municipal Employees:
***Scenario*: A local municipality sought to use ChatGPT to streamline citizen inquiries about utilities, property taxes, and public services.**
***Implementation*: The municipality developed a series of virtual training modules, teaching employees how to use and troubleshoot ChatGPT. This interactive training also included role-playing exercises where employees interacted with the system in real-time.**
***Impact*: Employees felt more confident in their ability to assist citizens using the system. They could redirect basic inquiries to ChatGPT, focusing their energies on more complex issues, leading to a 40% increase in operational efficiency.**

2. Cross-Training Workshops in Healthcare:
***Scenario*: A national health department implemented ChatGPT to answer queries related to health services, insurance, and public health campaigns.**
***Implementation*: The department organized cross-training workshops where IT professionals trained healthcare staff in the technical aspects of ChatGPT, while healthcare professionals trained IT teams about medical terminologies and health policies. This holistic approach ensured a comprehensive understanding of the system and its application.**

Impact: The effective collaboration reduced misunderstandings and system errors, leading to a 50% drop in inaccuracies in ChatGPT's responses to public queries.

3. University Collaborations for Advanced Training:
Scenario: A country's ministry of science and technology aimed to use ChatGPT for research inquiries, funding opportunities, and patent registrations.
Implementation: The ministry collaborated with top universities to create a curriculum for ChatGPT training. This collaboration provided advanced training sessions, integrating the latest AI research and technological insights into the training program.
Impact: The ministry saw a rise in successful research grant applications by 30%, as researchers could easily navigate funding opportunities using ChatGPT.

4. Feedback-Driven Training in Public Safety:
Scenario: A city's police department launched ChatGPT to assist citizens in reporting non-emergency issues, accessing public safety resources, and understanding local laws.
Implementation: The police department established a feedback mechanism where users could rate their interactions with ChatGPT. Monthly training sessions were organized based on this feedback, addressing any recurring issues or confusion among the staff.
Impact: The continuous feedback loop improved the accuracy and effectiveness of ChatGPT interactions, leading to a 60% increase in user satisfaction within six months.

5. AI Ethics Workshops for Decision Makers:
***Scenario*: The national government planned to deploy ChatGPT across various ministries for public interactions.**
***Implementation*: Recognizing the ethical challenges posed by AI, the government organized AI ethics workshops for senior officials and decision-makers. These sessions covered topics like data privacy, algorithmic bias, and responsible AI deployment.**
***Impact*: The workshops led to a more informed and cautious rollout of ChatGPT across government platforms. It ensured that the AI system aligned with ethical standards and public interest, fostering trust among citizens.**

These examples highlight the significance of tailored training programs and capacity-building initiatives in the successful deployment of AI technologies like ChatGPT in government operations. By investing in continuous learning and feedback mechanisms, governmental entities can ensure that their staff and the AI systems they utilize are both efficient and ethically sound.

1. Disaster Management:

With climate change intensifying, the occurrence of natural disasters is predicted to rise, making effective disaster management more crucial than ever. AI models like ChatGPT can play a significant role in enhancing these efforts. By processing large amounts of data from various sources, including weather forecasts, geological surveys, and social media feeds, ChatGPT could help in predicting potential disaster zones and providing early warnings, potentially saving lives and property. During disasters, ChatGPT can assist in coordinating response efforts by facilitating effective communication between different parties, ranging from emergency services to affected communities.

2. Education:

The future of education is likely to be increasingly digital and personalized, and here, ChatGPT could play a transformative role. It could assist in creating customized learning plans for students, factoring in their individual learning styles, pace, and interests. Moreover, it could serve as an intelligent tutor, providing students with instant, on-demand academic help, thereby bridging the gap in access to quality education and enhancing the overall learning experience.

3. Healthcare:
Healthcare is another sector where the applications of ChatGPT could be profound. It could assist in diagnosing diseases by analyzing patient symptoms and medical

history, as well as suggesting possible treatments based on latest medical research. Furthermore, it could be used to raise awareness about public health issues, disseminate health-related information, and remind citizens about important healthcare dates like vaccination schedules.

3. Public Engagement:

In the sphere of public engagement, ChatGPT could redefine how governments interact with their citizens. It could automate many public services, making them available 24/7 and more accessible. Additionally, it could be used to gather public opinion on various topics, providing valuable feedback to governments, and thereby increasing citizen participation in government decisions.

Looking ahead, the potential applications of AI technologies like ChatGPT in government are vast and varied. However, this future also brings with it new challenges and considerations. For instance, the use of AI in critical areas like healthcare or disaster management raises serious ethical and privacy issues, necessitating stringent safeguards. Moreover, as AI becomes more integrated in public services, governments need to ensure they are building an AI-ready workforce, and that their citizens are equipped with the necessary digital literacy.

In conclusion, while the future of ChatGPT in government holds immense promise, it's imperative to navigate this future with caution, responsibility, and a strong commitment to serving the public good. As governments around the world continue to explore and integrate AI into their services, they must ensure these advancements align with the principles of fairness, transparency, and accountability, with the aim of enhancing the efficiency, effectiveness, and inclusivity of public service.

As climate change intensifies and natural disasters become increasingly common, there is an urgent need for effective disaster management strategies. Leveraging artificial intelligence, specifically language models like ChatGPT, can significantly bolster these efforts.

Prediction and Early Warnings:

One of the primary ways ChatGPT can aid disaster management is through prediction and early warnings. A critical aspect of disaster management is the ability to anticipate disaster zones ahead of time to implement precautionary measures, prepare emergency responses, and potentially evacuate threatened populations.

ChatGPT can be trained to process a wide array of data — from weather patterns, seismic activity, and climate models to geospatial data and historical disaster data — to predict areas at high risk for various disasters. For instance, for hurricanes, AI can assess oceanic temperatures, atmospheric pressure changes, wind patterns, and historical hurricane paths to anticipate a hurricane's trajectory and potential landfall sites.

Once a high-risk area is identified, ChatGPT can aid in crafting effective early warning messages. By ensuring these messages are clear, understandable, and tailored to different populations (considering factors like age, language, and special needs), the AI can help ensure the highest possible number of people take necessary precautions or evacuate.

Disaster Response Coordination:

In the midst of a disaster, effective communication and coordination between different parties are vital. ChatGPT can assist by serving as a central communication hub, processing updates from field workers, emergency services, affected communities, and government bodies. It can help prioritize information, highlight urgent needs, and direct resources effectively. For instance, it can process updates from different sources to map out areas with the most urgent need for medical assistance, food, or evacuation support.

Furthermore, ChatGPT can provide real-time information and guidance to affected communities through easily accessible platforms like social media or messaging apps. This can range from guiding individuals to the nearest safe zone to providing first aid instructions.

Post-Disaster Analysis and Learning:

After a disaster, AI can help conduct a comprehensive post-disaster analysis. By processing data from the disaster response, it can identify what worked well, where the gaps were, and what needs improvement. These insights can be instrumental in refining disaster management strategies, enhancing preparedness for future disasters.

In conclusion, AI technologies like ChatGPT have significant potential in enhancing disaster management, from predicting disasters and facilitating early warnings to coordinating disaster response and driving post-disaster learning. However, their use in this context must be handled with care, ensuring accuracy of information, maintaining ethical use of data, and taking steps to avoid over-reliance on AI at the cost of human judgment and expertise.

The field of education stands to benefit significantly from the application of AI models like ChatGPT. These AI systems can not only optimize the teaching process but also offer individualized learning experiences to students, enhancing educational outcomes significantly.

Personalized Learning:

Education is not a one-size-fits-all endeavor. Every student has unique learning preferences, pace, and interests. Personalized learning, which tailors educational experiences to cater to individual students' needs, is increasingly recognized as a crucial aspect of effective education. However, creating customized learning plans for each student can be an arduous task for educators. This is where ChatGPT can assist.

By analyzing a student's performance data, interests, strengths, and weaknesses, ChatGPT can generate personalized learning plans. For instance, if a student excels in visual learning but struggles with textual materials, the AI can suggest more visual content. If a student demonstrates keen interest in space science, the AI can recommend resources or projects related to that topic. This personalization can make learning more engaging and effective for students.

Intelligent Tutoring:

ChatGPT can also serve as an 'intelligent tutor' for students. Traditional tutoring requires coordinating schedules between the tutor and the student, which can be challenging. However, an AI tutor can be available 24/7, providing immediate, on-demand academic support.

ChatGPT can answer student queries, explain complex concepts, guide students through problem-solving processes, and provide instant feedback on assignments. Its ability to process natural language means it can interact with students in a conversational manner, making the tutoring experience more engaging.

Educational Administration:

In addition to aiding learning, ChatGPT can also assist in educational administration. For instance, it can help automate tasks like scheduling, grading, and reporting, saving valuable time for educators. It can also analyze data to identify trends, such as subjects where students typically struggle, allowing educators to adjust their teaching strategies accordingly.

In conclusion, AI technologies like ChatGPT have immense potential to revolutionize education, from personalizing learning experiences to facilitating on-demand tutoring and optimizing educational administration. However, as AI systems are integrated into education, it's essential to consider ethical and privacy considerations, such as the use of student data, to ensure that these technologies are used responsibly and effectively.

Diagnosis and Treatment:

In the field of healthcare, AI models like ChatGPT could be instrumental in aiding disease diagnosis and treatment. It can be used to analyze patient symptoms, medical history, and relevant scientific literature to generate a list of possible diagnoses. By examining patterns in the data, it could help identify rare or complex conditions that might otherwise be overlooked.

Beyond diagnosis, ChatGPT can also assist in suggesting potential treatments based on patient information and medical guidelines. For example, it could recommend a certain medication for a patient with a specific condition, taking into account factors like the patient's age, other medications they are taking, and any pre-existing conditions they may have. This could support doctors in making informed treatment decisions.

It's important to note that while ChatGPT can assist in diagnosis and treatment, it should not replace the judgement of medical professionals. Its suggestions should be taken as additional information that doctors can consider when making their decisions.

Health Education and Information Dissemination:

ChatGPT can play a significant role in health education and dissemination of health-related information. It can be used to generate easy-to-understand content about various health topics, helping to raise public awareness about important health issues.

For instance, during a public health crisis like the COVID-19 pandemic, ChatGPT could generate informative content about the virus, preventative measures, and the latest scientific research. This could help ensure that citizens are well-informed and can take necessary precautions to protect their health.

Healthcare Reminders:

ChatGPT can also serve as an automated reminder system for important healthcare dates. For example, it can remind citizens about upcoming appointments, medication schedules, or vaccination dates. These reminders can help improve adherence to medical advice and ensure that citizens don't miss important healthcare services.

Future Possibilities:

With the continuing advancements in AI and machine learning technologies, the potential applications of AI models like ChatGPT in healthcare are vast. Future versions of ChatGPT could potentially understand and generate more complex medical content, assist in medical research, and even support mental health services by providing automated cognitive behavioral therapy.

However, as with any application of AI in sensitive areas like healthcare, it's crucial to consider ethical and privacy implications. AI systems should always be used responsibly, and their outputs should be interpreted with care, especially when they pertain to health outcomes.

Automating Public Services:

One of the major potential applications of ChatGPT in government lies in automating public services. With its capacity to understand and generate human-like text, ChatGPT could be used to handle many routine interactions with the public, such as answering inquiries, processing requests, or providing information.

By automating these services, governments can make them available 24/7, increasing their accessibility. This could be particularly beneficial for citizens who may have difficulty accessing services during regular business hours, such as those who work unconventional hours or live in different time zones.

Moreover, automation can help improve the speed and efficiency of service delivery. For example, instead of waiting for a human operator to respond, citizens could get immediate responses from ChatGPT. This could reduce waiting times and improve citizen satisfaction with government services.

Gathering Public Opinion:

ChatGPT can also assist governments in gathering public opinion. It could be used to conduct automated surveys or polls on various topics, ranging from public policy to social issues. With its natural language processing capabilities, it could even analyze open-ended responses, providing governments with more nuanced insights into public sentiment.

Furthermore, ChatGPT could facilitate public consultations, allowing more citizens to have a say in government decisions. For instance, it could generate summaries of public feedback on proposed policies, helping policy makers understand the public's views and concerns.

By using AI technologies like ChatGPT to gather public opinion, governments can make their decision-making processes more transparent and inclusive, fostering greater public trust and participation.

Future Possibilities:

Looking ahead, the potential applications of ChatGPT in public engagement are vast. As the technology evolves, it could handle more complex interactions, provide more personalized services, and even facilitate real-time, AI-mediated dialogues between governments and their citizens.

However, as with all uses of AI in government, it's essential to balance the benefits with potential risks. Ensuring the privacy and security of citizen data, preventing AI bias, and maintaining the accountability and transparency of AI-mediated interactions should be top priorities as governments increase their use of AI in public engagement.

Looking ahead, the future of government operations could be significantly transformed by the integration of AI technologies like ChatGPT. From predictive analytics in disaster management to personalized learning in education, and from automated public services to data-driven healthcare, the potential applications are vast and varied.

Yet, as we move into this future, it is crucial to navigate the new challenges and considerations it brings. For example, the use of AI in sensitive and critical areas such as healthcare or disaster management not only has the potential to revolutionize these sectors but also raises significant ethical questions. Issues surrounding data privacy, informed consent, transparency, and accountability become even more critical in these contexts. As such, the implementation of AI technologies must be guided by robust ethical principles and stringent safeguards to ensure that the technology is used responsibly and that the rights and interests of individuals are protected.

Moreover, the increasing prevalence of AI necessitates a shift in the skills required by the workforce. Governments will need to invest in building an AI-ready workforce that can effectively leverage AI technologies. This might involve initiatives such as AI-focused training programs, collaborations with educational institutions and tech companies, and policies to attract and retain AI talent.

In addition, as AI becomes more integrated into everyday life, there is a need to ensure that citizens are equipped with the necessary digital literacy to engage with AI technologies. This includes understanding how AI systems work, the data they use, the decisions they make, and the potential risks they pose. By fostering digital literacy, governments can empower their citizens to navigate the

digital world safely and effectively, and to make informed decisions about their interactions with AI.
Finally, it's important to remember that the future of AI in government isn't solely dependent on technological advancements; it's equally about people – the policy makers who guide the use of AI, the personnel who implement it, and the citizens who interact with it. It's about ensuring that the use of AI serves the public interest, enhances the quality of government services, and ultimately, improves the lives of citizens. As we move forward, these should be the guiding principles in our journey towards an AI-enabled future.

In conclusion, the future of ChatGPT and similar AI technologies in government holds immense promise. The potential applications across various sectors – disaster management, education, healthcare, public engagement, and more – point towards a future where public services are significantly enhanced and made more accessible and efficient. It's an exciting vision, where technology and governance come together to create a more responsive, effective, and inclusive government.

However, with these advancements come new challenges and ethical considerations. As we navigate this future, it is imperative that we do so with caution and responsibility, ensuring that the rights, safety, and well-being of individuals are paramount. The utilization of AI in government should not be a matter of deploying the most advanced technologies, but rather deploying the right technologies in the right way, with a strong commitment to serving the public good.

Governments must balance the potential benefits of AI with the risks it poses. This requires robust legal and ethical frameworks, rigorous oversight, and constant vigilance. Furthermore, it necessitates an investment in people – in building an AI-ready workforce and in fostering an AI-literate society.

Moreover, it's critical that the implementation of AI in government be an inclusive process, involving not only policy makers and technologists, but also the wider public. The voices, perspectives, and interests of citizens should inform the ways in which AI is used in government, ensuring that the technology serves the needs and interests of all, not just a few.

As governments around the world continue to explore and integrate AI into their services, these considerations should be at the forefront. The goal should be a future where AI technologies like ChatGPT are harnessed responsibly and ethically to enhance the efficiency, effectiveness, and equity of public service. This is a future worth striving for, a future where technology and governance work hand in hand to improve the lives of citizens and create a more just and inclusive society.

EXAMPLES:

1. Disaster Prediction and Real-Time Aid Allocation:
***Scenario*: A coastal city, prone to cyclones and flooding, integrates ChatGPT into its disaster management department.**
***Prediction*: Advanced AI, with the ability to process massive datasets in real-time, will predict cyclone paths and flood-prone zones with increasing accuracy. In**

conjunction with ChatGPT, real-time communication systems can be developed to immediately alert residents in danger zones. Moreover, ChatGPT can coordinate the allocation of resources, like medical aid or food supplies, based on dynamic demand during the disaster.
Potential Impact: Rapid response times, improved allocation of resources, and better-informed citizens lead to significantly reduced casualties and property damage.

2. Personalized Learning Pathways in Education:
Scenario: A national education board introduces ChatGPT to assist in the digitization of their curriculum and student assistance.
Prediction: Going beyond just being an information provider, ChatGPT could evolve to create highly personalized learning pathways. By analyzing a student's strengths, weaknesses, interests, and learning speed, the AI can suggest tailored lesson plans, additional resources for difficult topics, or even potential career paths.
Potential Impact: Increased student engagement, higher retention rates, and a shift towards truly personalized education which caters to individual student needs.

3. Virtual Health Assistants for Remote Areas:
Scenario: A country with vast rural landscapes and limited medical facilities in these areas employs ChatGPT in its primary healthcare initiative.
Prediction: ChatGPT, equipped with advanced medical databases and diagnostic algorithms, becomes a primary health consultant in remote locations. Rural residents can discuss their symptoms with the system, receive preliminary diagnoses, and be directed to the nearest medical facility if required. Furthermore, the AI can

provide medication reminders, vaccination schedules, and health tips.
Potential Impact: Improved healthcare access for rural populations, early detection of diseases, and better-informed patients leading to overall better public health.

4. Direct Democracy and Policy Feedback:
Scenario: A city government aims to increase public participation in its policy-making process.
Prediction: Using ChatGPT, governments could create platforms where citizens can voice their opinions on policy proposals. The AI can then process thousands of responses to extract meaningful insights, gauge public sentiment, and even suggest modifications based on collective intelligence.
Potential Impact: Policies that better reflect the will and needs of the people, increased trust in governance, and a more involved and informed citizenry.

5. Cross-Departmental Integration and Efficiency:
Scenario: A national government seeks to streamline its operations, reduce bureaucracy, and improve inter-departmental communication.
Prediction: ChatGPT, combined with integrated governmental databases, can act as a mediator between departments. For instance, when a new infrastructure project is proposed, ChatGPT can instantly pull environmental assessments, budget allocations, and legal clearances from respective departments, significantly speeding up the approval process.
Potential Impact: More efficient governmental operations, reduced red tape, faster project completions, and increased inter-departmental collaboration.

Chapter 9's foresight into the application of ChatGPT in various governmental sectors hints at a future where AI isn't just an assistant but a cornerstone of effective, efficient, and inclusive governance. The examples elucidate the pivotal role AI could play in reshaping public services and the broader relationship between citizens and their government.

CHAPTER 10: CONCLUSION AND NEXT STEPS

The final chapter sums up the key points discussed in previous chapters. It provides guidance on formulating a roadmap for ChatGPT implementation, maintaining the system, and iterating improvements based on experiences and outcomes.

This concluding chapter offers a reflection on the myriad aspects of integrating ChatGPT into governmental operations and its potential future implications. We embarked on this journey by understanding the basics of artificial intelligence and the capabilities of ChatGPT, its potential benefits, and its applicability within the public sector. As we continued, we laid out the practical considerations, challenges, ethical implications, and the principles of Responsible AI that are critical in implementing such advanced technology in government functions.

ChatGPT has the potential to revolutionize various sectors of government operations - from improving the speed and efficiency of service delivery to providing personalized citizen experiences. These benefits, however, come with challenges that need to be addressed proactively. These include the risk of data bias, privacy concerns, and the need for transparency in AI decisions, to name a few. Addressing these challenges is not a one-time task but a continuous process that requires a commitment to Responsible AI principles. We explored this concept in detail, emphasizing the need for fairness, transparency, privacy, security, and accountability in AI applications.

Furthermore, we delved into the nuts and bolts of integrating ChatGPT into government operations. We provided guidance on selecting suitable tasks for AI, implementing the system, and ensuring its smooth operation. We emphasized the importance of training and capacity building, highlighting the need for comprehensive training programs, addressing skill gaps, and fostering an AI-positive culture within the government.

Looking into the future, we explored potential advancements and applications of ChatGPT in various sectors of government, from disaster management to education and healthcare. We envisaged a future where AI plays an integral role in public service delivery, yet cautioned against the ethical dilemmas and challenges that such a future could bring.

In this final chapter, we emphasize that the journey of AI implementation is continuous and iterative. It starts with strategic planning and thoughtful implementation but extends to regular monitoring, evaluation, and improvement. It requires not just the technical knowledge to use AI, but also the ethical understanding to use it responsibly. It demands that we balance the drive for efficiency and innovation with a steadfast commitment to fairness, transparency, and accountability.

As governments around the world continue to explore and embrace AI technologies like ChatGPT, they need to keep these considerations at the forefront. The potential of AI is immense, but so too is the responsibility that comes with it. Guided by the principles of Responsible AI and a commitment to public service, governments can harness the power of AI to improve their operations, serve their citizens better, and build a future where technology truly serves the public good.

As we conclude this exploration of ChatGPT in government, we must underscore that the journey towards the effective implementation of artificial intelligence in public service is an ongoing one. The continuous nature of this process necessitates the creation of a comprehensive roadmap for implementation, regular maintenance and system updates, and the ability to iterate improvements based on experiences and outcomes.

Formulating a roadmap: The first step towards integrating ChatGPT in government involves creating a strategic plan that outlines its implementation. This roadmap should articulate clear goals and objectives, identify key tasks suitable for AI, and define the roles and responsibilities of various stakeholders. It should also include provisions for training government personnel and building AI capacity. Equally important is outlining a plan for dealing with potential challenges, from technical glitches to ethical dilemmas, that may arise during implementation.

Maintaining the system: The maintenance of an AI system like ChatGPT is crucial for its smooth operation. It includes regularly updating the system to incorporate the latest AI advancements and ensuring that it continues to meet its intended objectives. Equally important is safeguarding the system against potential security threats and ensuring that it complies with privacy regulations. This process requires the combined effort of AI specialists, IT personnel, and policy-makers.

Iterating improvements: One of the greatest advantages of AI systems is their ability to learn and improve over time. Governments should harness this potential by continually monitoring the performance of ChatGPT, collecting feedback from its users, and making necessary adjustments. This could involve enhancing the system's capabilities, improving its user interface, or addressing any biases in its outputs.

The future of ChatGPT in government looks promising. But to harness this promise, governments need to approach AI with a mindset of continual learning and improvement. They need to be willing to adapt, innovate, and iterate, all the while keeping a steadfast commitment to responsible and ethical AI use. The journey of AI implementation is not always smooth, but with careful planning, diligent maintenance, and a willingness to learn from experiences and outcomes, it is a journey that holds the potential to significantly enhance public service delivery and citizen satisfaction.

Formulating a roadmap for ChatGPT implementation is an essential first step to transitioning towards a more AI-infused government operation. This strategic plan should outline the primary stages of the project and define both the micro and macro objectives of each stage. It should act as a blueprint to guide the project from its inception to its ultimate integration.

Planning: The initial stage of the roadmap should include identifying the key areas of government operations where ChatGPT can be deployed. This could be responding to public inquiries, assisting in policy making, or streamlining internal communication. Stakeholders need to define what success looks like for each of these areas, and these definitions should be aligned with broader organizational objectives.

Setup: Once the key areas are identified, the next step in the roadmap is setting up the system. This involves customizing ChatGPT to meet specific needs, integrating it with existing systems, and ensuring data privacy and security measures are in place.

Deployment: This stage of the roadmap should focus on launching the AI system. It should outline the processes for training users, establishing feedback channels, and rolling out the system in a phased manner to handle potential challenges better.

Evaluation: After deployment, it's important to have a plan for monitoring and evaluating the performance of ChatGPT. The roadmap should detail how performance indicators will be measured, how regular audits will be conducted, and how user feedback will be collected and analyzed.

Continual improvement: Lastly, the roadmap should plan for the ongoing improvement of ChatGPT. This involves continuously monitoring its performance, making necessary adjustments based on feedback and audit results, and staying updated with the latest developments in AI technology.

The roadmap should be flexible and adaptive, able to accommodate changes as the implementation process progresses. It's important to review and revise the roadmap regularly to reflect new insights, changing circumstances, or shifts in organizational priorities.

As we conclude, it's important to recognize that incorporating ChatGPT into government operations is not just a technological leap, but a significant step towards creating more efficient, responsive, and citizen-centered public services. The potential of AI technologies to transform how governments work and serve citizens is indeed immense. Yet, it's not without challenges and considerations.

The integration of ChatGPT into government operations needs meticulous planning and a clear vision of the intended goals. A well-defined roadmap, as discussed, can provide structure to this process and guide the progress. Importantly, the implementation is not a one-time affair, but rather a continuous journey. Regular monitoring and evaluation, coupled with continuous improvements based on feedback and audits, are vital to ensure the system remains effective and serves its intended purpose. Further, it's essential to remember that the integration of AI into government should always adhere to Responsible AI principles. This includes ensuring transparency, fairness, privacy, security, and accountability in the use of AI. The goal should be to use AI as a tool to augment human capabilities, enhance public service, and foster public trust.

As AI technologies continue to advance and their applications become more widespread, these principles and practices will be key to achieving a responsible, effective, and ethical use of AI in government. The journey of integrating ChatGPT into government operations has just begun, and as we navigate this path, we must strive to ensure that AI serves the public good. It's indeed an exciting future, one that holds the promise of a more efficient, effective, and citizen-centric government.

EXAMPLES:

1. Implementation of AI in Rural Health Clinics:
***Scenario*: A government aims to improve healthcare access and quality in its remote villages.**
***Roadmap & Implementation*: The government initiates pilot projects in select villages, providing clinics with ChatGPT-equipped devices. Local healthcare workers are trained to use the system, which aids in primary diagnoses, recommends treatments, and connects patients with specialists in urban centers via telehealth. Based on the feedback from these pilots, necessary iterations are made before wider-scale implementation.**
***Outcome*: Improved healthcare availability, reduced misdiagnoses, and the ability for remote populations to access specialist consultations without long travels.**

2. ChatGPT in E-Governance Platforms:
***Scenario*: A city council wants to enhance its e-governance portal to handle queries and process requests faster.**
***Roadmap & Implementation*: The city integrates ChatGPT into its online portal. The AI assists in auto-filling forms based on user queries, explaining governmental processes,**

or redirecting users to appropriate departments. Periodic audits and user feedback sessions are scheduled to understand the AI's efficiency and areas of improvement.
Outcome: Reduced wait times, increased user satisfaction, and a significant reduction in manual administrative work.

3. Enhancing Education through Virtual Tutors:
Scenario: A state education board seeks to supplement its teaching force with virtual tutors, especially for subjects with teacher shortages.
Roadmap & Implementation: Schools are equipped with AI-powered terminals. Students can approach ChatGPT with subject-related queries, homework help, or even career advice. The system's responses and interactions are monitored for quality, and teachers provide feedback to refine the AI's tutoring methods.
Outcome: Improved student performance, reduced dependency on a single teacher, and personalized assistance leading to more engaged students.

4. Public Safety and Disaster Response:
Scenario: A coastal state often faces natural disasters and wants a real-time response system.
Roadmap & Implementation: The state integrates ChatGPT with its emergency response system. The AI processes real-time data from weather stations, satellite imagery, and ground reports. It predicts potential disaster zones and coordinates with emergency services, dispatching aid and resources efficiently. The state continually refines the system based on each disaster response to enhance accuracy and efficiency.

Outcome: **Faster response times during disasters, better resource allocation, and a significant reduction in casualties.**

5. Enhancing Public Transport through AI:
Scenario: **A metropolitan city wants to improve its public transportation system's efficiency and user-friendliness.**
Roadmap & Implementation: **The city introduces ChatGPT-powered kiosks at major transport hubs. Commuters can inquire about routes, delays, alternative transport methods, or lodge complaints. The AI also predicts transport demands based on various factors, helping the city in dynamic resource allocation. Regular feedback loops with commuters and transport staff help in fine-tuning the AI's suggestions and functionality.**
Outcome: **Improved public transport efficiency, reduced waiting times, and an enhanced commuter experience.**

Chapter 10, with its focus on pragmatic implementation and iterative improvement, underscores the importance of continuous monitoring, feedback, and adaptation. By doing so, governments can ensure that the integration of technologies like ChatGPT remains aligned with the needs of the public and the evolving dynamics of governance.

AUTHOR'S ENDNOTE"

This book was written by the author, collaboratively with a generative AI system, Chat GPT.